Agnes Blake Poor

Brothers and Strangers

Agnes Blake Poor

Brothers and Strangers

ISBN/EAN: 9783337139773

Printed in Europe, USA, Canada, Australia, Japan

Cover: Foto ©ninafisch / pixelio.de

More available books at **www.hansebooks.com**

BROTHERS AND STRANGERS

BROTHERS AND STRANGERS

BY

AGNES BLAKE POOR

(DOROTHY PRESCOTT)

"The tallest flower that skyward rears its head,
Grows from the common earth, and there must shed
Its delicate petals."
Hartley Coleridge.

BOSTON
ROBERTS BROTHERS
1893

Copyright, 1893,
BY ROBERTS BROTHERS.

University Press:
JOHN WILSON AND SON, CAMBRIDGE, U.S.A.

BROTHERS AND STRANGERS.

CHAPTER I.

FROM MRS. BUTLER TO ARTHUR BUTLER.

LIVERPOOL, N Y., April 5, 188-.

MY DEAR SON, — I was glad to hear by your last that you were in good health, and that your worldly prospects look so bright. I only hope you spare some time to reflect on the great concern of your soul's salvation. Believe, oh, believe an affectionate mother's word, that it is best to seek the Lord in your youth. It is a constant grief to me that only *one* of my dear children as yet cherishes a hope; but my daily prayer is that I may meet you all in heaven. I have much anxiety and trouble at present, and am very fatigued; but I know that in this world I must expect tribulation. I wrote you fully after the arrival of dear Orlando and his little family, and dropped you a postal telling of the birth of Ida's babe, but have not had time to write a letter since, though I have commenced several. It is a lovely but very delicate infant, and its dear young mother was so sick at the time of its birth that she has never been able to nurse it, and we have to bring it up on the bottle, and it is very hard to find a food that will agree with it; its cries are distressing. You will be much pleased to hear that Orlando and Ida have decided to name it Arthur, after you. The other children are very well, though they have frequent colds and attacks of indigestion.

Almira was here last week with her dear little girl; she said John was too busy to come. They are all well, and John seems uncommonly prosperous. Almira brought me a very lovely cream pitcher from the store, that must have been worth at least seventy-five cents at sale. I thought she was dressed too much for a church member, and disliked to see the little Laurea so expensively arrayed. I felt it my duty to speak about it, and hope what I said may have a good effect. They have asked me to make them a visit, and I shall go [D. V.] as soon as Orlando has found another parish. He has not been able to make any effort to seek for one, he has been so occupied with the care of his wife. Oh, I forgot to tell you that dear Jonah is here too. He has left his place, and does not wish to return to Cazenovia. I am sorry he could not have stayed on a little longer, but the food they gave him was very poor, and Jonah is not very well, though he looks healthy. I am afraid John will not be able to find him another place; could you not get something for him to do in Boston? I think he might like it there better, and then you could look after him. I dread his being exposed to the temptations of a city, more especially as he is not yet a professing Christian. May that blest day soon arrive! I have no girl at present, and find the work rather beyond my strength, though Flora, Ida's sister, who came with them, does all she can to help me. She is a very sweet girl. Of course my expenses are much increased with so large a family, and I must beg you, if it is not too much trouble, and you can *perfectly* well afford it, to send me a small sum in addition to the regular allowance you so kindly make me, as I dread the disgrace of getting into debt more than anything else. Orlando and Jonah send their love, and I am

Your affectionate mother.

Mr. ARTHUR BUTLER,
Ames Building, Boston, Mass.

Arthur Butler was not a man given to show his feelings in his face; but as he slowly read for the second time the above letter, written in a fine copy-book hand, and closely squeezed on to the smallest possible scrap of thin blue ruled paper, he looked gloomy enough. He was not at his office, to which it was addressed, but in his apartment in a large old-fashioned house on the eastern slope of Beacon Hill, with a view, over the crest, of the waving trees on the Common. It was a handsome room, and though somewhat bare to a modern eye, everything in it, the furniture, the books, the pictures, were good of their kind. The care which was evidently taken of them was greater than masculine nature is generally willing to bestow on its belongings, and seemed to mark their owner as not only a bachelor, but an old one. Arthur, however, was but two-and-thirty. He had come up town earlier than usual for a particular reason; but though pressed for time, he sat down, and deliberately, but with no hesitation, wrote an answer on the thickest of white paper, in a firm, decided hand, legible, but characteristic; read it over once, and then without making addition or erasure, folded, sealed, and addressed it. It ran as follows: —

Beacon Street, BOSTON, April 7, 188-.

MY DEAR MOTHER, — I am sorry that you feel under the necessity of applying to me for further assistance. You know that I have never grudged you anything that was in my power to give. I did not expect that John, so long as you declined his offer of a home in his family, would feel called upon to do anything for you outside; but I did not wonder that you preferred one of your own, and as soon as I was able, I established you in your own old house, and insured you a comfortable income, safe from anything that might happen to me. It was enough to enable you to live in comfort in Liverpool, and keep a servant; but I certainly did not allow for its supporting seven other people in addition. If Orlando chose to marry young and burden himself with children before he was able properly to maintain them, he ought not to look to me to help him out. I am older than he, and if I had the means, might very likely wish to marry myself, which I shall not be able to do if I am to be at the expense of supporting him and his family, including, it seems, his wife's relations. As for Jonah, he ought at least to be able to take care of himself, when nothing more is expected of him. They should consider that it is you on whom they are living, and that what they take diminishes your comfort by just so much; and if they have any manly feeling left they will bestir themselves a little.

Under the circumstances, I do not think it wise to increase your income; it would only be giving it to them, and that is the same thing as throwing it into the sea. I have already done all I can for them, and more than they had a right to look for. I am very sorry that you should be exposed to mortifications and annoyances which you ought to have been spared. I presume from what you say that you have already incurred debts, and look to me to pay them. I shall only be willing to do this upon the security that I shall not be liable to be called on again. I think the best thing to do will be for me to run on and see how things stand with my own eyes. I can leave here Thursday in the night train, and stay over Sunday with you. I will stop in Syracuse and talk with John about it; but I want you to understand that I have not the least desire that you should live with him if you do not wish to. Perhaps it will be best for you to let the house and board somewhere; but we can decide this when we meet.

Do not trouble yourself to prepare a room for me; you must be full enough, and I can put up at Kemp's for the brief time of my stay.

Believe me ever your affectionate son,

ARTHUR BUTLER.

Mrs. JOHN BUTLER,
   Liverpool, New York.

After finishing his letter, and dressing himself with scrupulous attention, he went out, carrying it in his hand. Light as a feather as it was, it, or what it recalled, weighed like lead on his heart. Arthur Butler was not, strictly speaking, handsome, but he drew attention in any crowd, and was looked at twice by every woman he met; for a certain air of distinction, that lay not so much in the careful but easy elegance of his toilet and all his appurtenances, and the grace with which he carried his slight but muscular figure, looking tall, though not much over middle height, as in an elevation of expression which, with the low, slow, perfect modulations of his voice, and his condescending courtesy of manner, impressed those who met him deeply, and more or less pleasantly according as he himself was pleased or displeased, and made them say of him, with varying significance, that he was a " born and bred aristocrat."

He never looked more so than at this moment, with his face darkened by a not unbecoming shadow. It was a fine example of the irony of nature that his thoughts were running on his boyish days, when he used, cold and hungry, or hot and thirsty, according to the season, to peddle baskets, the staple of Liverpool, made by himself, through the streets of the neighboring city of Syracuse. With the capacity of memory to take in a world at once, he saw himself in a dozen different phases, — sweeping out the village grocery store, and carrying home parcels in the intervals of the district school; grown older, doing similar work in a country lawyer's office, and picking up what law he could between times; putting himself through college, teaching in all his vacations, and bookkeeping, copying, and what not, in all his odd moments, while he won scholarship after scholarship by sheer hard work, for he was not quick; all this since he had made up his mind, a little, poorly fed, half clad boy of seven years old, the day his father's shabby funeral train had left behind an almost empty house, that he would never be a poor man.

The opening and sharp sudden snap of a post-box lid dispersed with a start the dreams of his boyish home, and as he walked with a quickened step down the long slope of Beacon Hill, toward the setting sun, the clouds rolled away from his face as from his heart, both set forward to an anticipated pleasure. He crossed the Public Garden, fresh with budding leaves and bright with spring flowers, and stopped in Commonwealth Avenue, where the doors of the great Griswold house were thrown wide open to a surging crowd, and the Griswolds, devoutly hoping that no one had by any ill chance been forgotten, were receiving and "doing up" all who could by any possibility consider themselves entitled to be asked to meet a son of the house and his bride from New York. As is usually the case at such assemblages, the mixture was a promiscuous one, — of every set, and some of no set at all. People ran against those they had long thought dead, exchanged affectionate greetings with those with whom they were not on speaking terms, cut their own uncles and aunts, overlooked those they were looking for, and miscalled half their friends. No such mistakes were made by Arthur Butler, or if made were never detected, as he threaded the crowd, grave, courteous, responsive, with a quick eye to recognize, and a few well chosen words for every one he knew. His acquaintance was numerous, if select, and he was greeted at every turn; but he could disengage himself from a conversation as easily as he could take it up. No one detained him long, nor indeed seemed to expect to do so; and when he finally made his way to the goal of his wishes at the side of Miss Sophy Curtis, it was with the tacit approval of all lookers-on, and of the young lady herself, who looked up with a smile of welcome that gave its fairest aspect to her honest, homely face.

Miss Curtis was not beautiful, nor very

young, nor very rich, nor very fashionable, and Arthur Butler was not at all in love with her; but he thoroughly liked, respected, and admired her, and hoped to make her his wife. Fashion he did not care for, — it implied an uneasy strain to keep one's self before the public eye, which shocked his fastidious taste, and to which the comfortable, sheltered, easy, well-assured position of the Curtises was infinitely superior. If he disliked anything worse than the hard wooden made-up faces, the stiff costly raiment, the loud flippant repartees of the married women of uncertain age, precious in their ugliness as Byzantine Madonnas, who led the present style, it was to see the unmarried girls trying to imitate them. As to beauty, he had little to say to the blushing rose-buds of the garden, who were, indeed, somewhat afraid of him. The frank cordiality of Sophy's plain pleasant face, and the through and through freshness and neatness of her simple but well chosen attire, which threw an air of refinement over her vigorous health, satisfied him thoroughly. He had too much pride to relish the idea of marrying an heiress; but her inheritance as one of the many children of a man well-to-do in business, with a comfortable property to fall back upon, would help, not encumber, a husband's ambition. Then she had further expectations, not sufficiently certain to mark him as a fortune-hunter, and by a curious conjunction of circumstances so much more likely to be gratified if she married him than if she married anybody else that the match might be said to be for her interest, too. Altogether the thing had a fitness about it which almost tempted him to believe that the woman brought up in luxurious ease, to the best the world could give, widely travelled, assiduously taught, and the man who had fought every inch of his toilsome way upward, were " predestinated mates."

As they stood together now, he looked the finer clay than she. His grand air was his great charm in Sophy's eyes. She knew that, as the common phrase goes, he had made himself; but then, so had her own grandfather; and her critical faculty was not sufficiently developed to weigh the difference in antecedents and starting-point between a boy growing up sixty years ago on his father's well-tilled farm on the richest lands in Vermont, and one of the present day left twenty-five years ago fatherless and penniless in a little town in New York. There was no design at concealment on Arthur's part; the reason that he so seldom mentioned his relations was simply that they did not interest him, and he did not expect them to interest other people; and Sophy, when she thought of them at all, classed them with the distant Curtis cousins in Vermont, who were mostly plain, well-to-do people of good standing in their respective towns and villages, and with whom the wealthy Boston branch of the family, though meeting them but seldom, was on the very best of terms.

"Have you been able to find the maps?" she asked with interest, as soon as the first greetings had been exchanged.

"Yes, very nice ones, I should think, — one of the world on Mercator's projection, and one in hemispheres, — both on a good large scale."

"Thank you; that will be delightful; and we will begin with the Norsemen and Leif Eiriksson. I will get out some of Cousin Rachel's Norwegian photographs."

"And I can borrow some good ones of Iceland and Greenland from Mr. Hitchcock, who went in the Bowdoin College Expedition."

"How very kind! I will take the greatest

care of them; but we may have to keep them over two times, if he does not mind."

"Would you mind if I asked Mr. Hitchcock to come and explain them himself next Friday? I fear I cannot come that evening."

"Oh, why not?" asked the young lady, surprised; "where are you going? I beg your pardon," she added, hastily, correcting herself.

"I find I must go to Liverpool to see my mother. I am afraid she is not very well."

"I am very sorry," said Sophy, with a look of just the proper amount of concern.

"It is nothing serious, I hope; but I cannot be easy without seeing for myself."

"No, indeed!" said Sophy, who supposed Arthur Butler, in addition to all his other virtues, must be the most devoted of sons. "We shall miss you; but of course it cannot be helped. Perhaps before you leave, you will give us some idea of how far we have to go, for I am afraid I can never manage Eirik the Red without you; but I dare say we can fill up one evening with the early Norsemen and the settlement of Iceland."

"Miss Curtis was so kind as to ask me to dinner, to-night, and she added to her kindness by telling me I was to meet you. I shall be very glad to help you in any way."

"That will be very nice," said the young lady, frankly; "and you will be back, perhaps, before the next time."

"I shall come back as soon as I possibly can, you may be very sure."

There was something so meaning in his tone that Sophy colored all over; her healthy, blooming face lacked the delicacy of texture which makes a blush really becoming; but still the slight confusion which softened her usually self-reliant, unsentimental expression, was pleasing in the young man's eyes. Perhaps, too, she reaped some advantage from her lover's family troubles, which by throwing difficulties in the way, fostered that lover-like impatience which might otherwise have hardly enlivened the course of so smooth and satisfactory a wooing. He had been feeling his way with caution, but now he began to see it so clear before him, that were it not for this vexatious going to Liverpool hanging over him, he might almost have been tempted to speak out plainly now. They had stopped to hold their little parley, and the surging crowd, impatient of any obstacle, had swept them a little out of the direct route to the tea-room, into a corner recess, where they were practically free from being overheard or interrupted; but it was not in his nature to trust to chance opportunities like this; he would have every advantage of place and time, particularly as the acceptance, which he without undue presumption expected, would at once entail a good deal of business.

Sophy asked for no more; he had said enough, and looked enough to make her content in waiting for his return; and there was a happy flutter in her voice as she said, "I think I must look for Cousin Rachel, now, for I am sure she must want to go — Ah, there she is!" as a lady on the other side of the room nodded to Arthur with a look of familiar acquaintance and pleased approval, while both young people did their best to join her with as little delay as possible. She was twenty-five years older than her young cousin, but was, even now, a much handsomer woman. Her tall well-rounded figure, thick silver-gray hair, fresh fair skin, fine eyes, fine teeth, all well preserved by unremitting care and the assistance of experts in every line of treatment, and set off by the rich, sombre, glowing hues of her dark red cashmere and velvet costume, gave the imposing effect of undecayed maturity. Her presence was no impediment to Arthur's love-making, — rather an incentive, though she was the real lady of his adoration.

CHAPTER II.

MISS RACHEL CURTIS was the first cousin of Sophy's father. Her own father, with his, had come to Boston from Vermont when young, and made very good fortunes in the grocery business; but the elder and leading partner of the firm had more largely increased his gains by investments, and while his brother had a large family, who married and had large families in their turn, he had left an only daughter, sole heiress to a property which, if not entitled to be called colossal, made a highly respectable figure in the Boston tax lists, invested as it now was in the best of real estate, bonds of the State of Massachusetts, Boston and Providence Railway, and other "gilt-edged" securities. She could spend money with a freedom and safety which the possessors of more unlimited wealth do not always enjoy. She was not born till her father was well advanced in years and prosperity, and had been left, still young, with her entire fortune under her own control; and she had never found any difficulty in managing the principal, or in spending the income so as to secure the largest possible amount of satisfaction for herself, and every one who came in contact with her, with entire independence as to what others thought she ought to do, or might do, or what they would do in her place. For society in general she cared but little, having never had any difficulty in surrounding herself with the particular society she best liked; and though good-natured, she was fastidious, for daughter of a grocer as she was, she had enough refinement and culture to serve for a royal princess, — perhaps for two.

Whether Miss Curtis had always been as thoroughly satisfied with her enviable place in the world as she now appeared to be, cannot with certainty be told. She had never shown the slightest eagerness to purchase position and rank at home or abroad, with her wealth; and it was never known that she had had any real love affair, though she had a very decided liking for the society of the other sex, which now showed itself in taking a friendly interest of a highly beneficent description in clever and attractive young men, who in their turn could often be useful to her. Of all these little harmless attachments the strongest was that which had drawn her to Arthur Butler, whose acquaintance she had made while he was still in college, at a rather older age than the average undergraduate. His good looks and good manners had pleased her, and the energy with which, as she discovered, he was struggling to educate himself under so many drawbacks won her respect and admiration. Gladly would she have done more to help him than his pride would allow, but no pride could refuse what she did give; she threw open to him her beautiful home, full of treasures of literature and art, introduced him to her friends, and in a hundred delicate ways gave sympathy, advice, encouragement. She helped him unobtrusively to business when he began to practise law, and the opening wedge once inserted, he was well able to get on. As eagerly did he seize every hint, every example of graceful and refined custom in Miss Curtis's sphere, and grasp, though lightly, at the delicate tendrils by whose aid, but without straining them, must be climbed the flowery steeps of society. For these chances he felt more grateful to her than for anything else she had done for him. Now, it seemed that he might be drawn yet nearer to her by relationship The Curtises, prosperous, content, and united, were not disposed to cavil at any disposal Rachel might make of her money, so long as the bulk of it remained in the family. It might suit her to divide it among her kinsfolk, or choose one as her heir; and in the latter case, Sophy, the oldest child of her favorite cousin and of the especial friend of her girlhood, named at her request after her own mother, and always distinguished by her particular regard, might well receive the preference. There is a natural wish to plan out the disposition of one's fortune as far as possible, and it might make some difference whom Sophy married; but if she married Arthur Butler, a favorite himself, their united claims would probably be irresistible. He would not need this added merit to recommend him to Sophy's parents. Good girl as she was, she had never been particularly admired in society, and was already beginning to feel the interest of an incipient maiden aunt in her prettier younger sister Rosamond's new establishment and new baby. She did not take this much to heart, nor did her parents for her. All their girls were well provided for, and need not marry unless they wished; but if they did wish to marry any well-favored, well-placed, well-spoken-of young man, they were sure of a kind consent and a generous fitting-out. Arthur's personal claims were beyond the common, and as to his family, they would make no difference; if undesirable, they were at a safe distance. The Curtis connection was so large that there was no need of increasing it, and Sophy would be glad to live among her own people, and belong to them. Her feelings were beginning to be plain enough even to herself. With a double share of modesty, half as woman, and half as her own individual self, she could no longer mistake Arthur's meaning. She had long known and always admired him, but she had never dreamed of him, nor indeed of any one else as a possible lover, and the joy was greater when the surprise came.

No one else saw it more plainly, or with more pleasure, than Rachel Curtis, who was quite as willing to be regarded in the light of an adopted mother as any one could be to have her. She was very dependent on the society and attentions of both Sophy and Arthur; and this was a sure way, and indeed the only way, of not losing either. She was no match-maker, but she felt a little harmless pride in the thought that the acquaintance had begun with her, and that she might be supposed to be an attraction, though a subsidiary one. She did not know how near she had come to being a principal in the affair, or dream that for some time Arthur had seriously revolved in his mind the question of proposing marriage to her; and that he had been deterred, not so much by the dread of the construction the world might place on his motives, though this was not without its weight; for he knew truly that into such love-making he could have thrown more personal devotion, and less self-interest, than into his present more apparently suitable aspirations; not so much by doubts of his ultimate success, for his suit once opened, he felt he had the will and power to carry it through; but from a terror of the beginning. Miss Curtis's first look of blank amazement, perhaps of ridicule, when he should have succeeded in making her understand what he meant, would keep rising before him. He had never found courage to encounter it, and had at last settled on what was safely within his reach, and the more ostensible choice. There would always be a little mixture of sentiment in his relations with his wife's aunt, all the more tender because of the marriage, and sure to please the future Mrs. Arthur Butler.

Miss Curtis, unsuspicious of all this, and with her future more full of promise than it is apt to be after the most prosperous life of fifty-two years, was the happiest of the little party of three, a most sociable one for that proverbially unfortunate number, which gathered round her dinner-table that night; she was certainly the liveliest. Arthur was grave, and Sophy quiet; but that was natural when they were to part, even for so short a time; and she thought that nothing could be prettier or in better taste than the courtship of her two model young people.

"Sophy tells me your mother is not well," said the hostess, in a tone of concern, as soon as they were fairly settled at the table.

"She is not really ill; but I fear that she is not comfortably situated, and that the others do not quite understand how to make her so."

"I am sure it will do her good to see you," said Miss Curtis, heartily; "and would you mind taking charge of a little present for her from me? It will not be a very large parcel," she added, laughing; "for I know how much men dislike that."

"Thank you. Of course I shall be only too happy to take anything you are so kind as to send."

"It is a great favorite of mine, and if she is confined to her room, perhaps she will enjoy having it by her."

"Your thinking of her will give her great pleasure, I know."

"You must tell us just how far to go on Friday," said Sophy, as her cousin was silent.

"I could write out a little outline for you to refer to, but there will be no need of it. You have planned out quite enough for one evening."

"The boys will miss you, I am sure; but I shall put them on their good behavior, by promising to report to you when you come back."

"Don't you think they improve?" asked Miss Curtis.

"Yes — I think there is some progress," said Arthur, doubtfully.

"Oh, I am sure there is!" cried Sophy. "Don't you remember how troublesome Willie MacIntyre used to be? And now he is so attentive. And those two little Rosenbaum boys, they were perfectly stolid, and now they do show a great deal of interest."

"They are interested enough, if that were all; but I should like to see them able to make themselves behave a little better when they are not being amused."

"Oh, poor little fellows! what can you expect? Just think what homes they come from. Willie's father is dead, and his mother has no control over her boys; she lets them roam the streets, and only frets at them in a way that is worse than saying nothing. I am sure it is ruining Allan."

"Yes," said Miss Curtis, "I wish we could have got any hold on Allan MacIntyre before he grew so wild. But I do not suppose he would come to the class, even if I dared risk him there, to injure the others, perhaps. You must try to get at him, Arthur; a man might do something with him."

The conversation ran on about the fruitful topic of the members of an evening class which Miss Curtis entertained weekly at her own house, selected from the most promising (not always the best-behaved) of the many poor boys in whom she took an interest. She made no distinctions; and French-Canadian, Irish, German, Italian, — even colored, of all shades, were impartially admitted; the only test being whether they enjoyed the entertainment provided for them, — at present a course of historical and geographical talks on the great discoverers of the world, — sufficiently to make them come regularly and listen with some attention. It had worked very well. The elegance of the surroundings, and Miss Curtis's commanding presence, tamed the boys down; Sophy, well trained by younger brothers, had a free, pleasant understanding with them which won their confidence; and Arthur's unwavering firmness under his quiet manner was a check on the unruly. He had the power of controlling others which comes with self-control; and his, as he used to think with pride, was absolute; it had been bought at the cost of too many hard knocks that must be silently borne.

He grew silent now while Miss Curtis and Sophy lingered on their favorite theme, the tastes and characters of the boys; for somehow when they were on this topic, his early memories grew stronger, and he always felt like one of the little ragamuffins, whose orphan state, and wretched home, and scant and starved condition, were the objects of so much compassion, — kind, but uncomprehending. They talked as those do who have never known what it is to want a meal; hardly what it is to eat a badly cooked one. The surroundings were perfect; no glare, no ostentation. The room was neither so bare as to look large, nor so crowded as to look small, but gave a sense of spaciousness and snugness at once. The soft, dispersed light; the faint fresh wafts of perfume from flowers, some seen, some unseen; the delicate preparations which gave the sense of taste a gratification not less refined; the quiet, easy serving, which anticipated every wish, — these were the luxuries which Arthur Butler prized. He had always craved them even when he knew less about them. If one only had them, he thought, it might be possible to do without gold-plate or Bohemian glass; but they were not less expensive. Wax candles and hot-house roses cost a great deal of money; and so did such servants as Miss Curtis employed. Indeed, so did Miss Curtis and Sophy themselves. Their dresses looked simple enough, but the absolute unconsciousness with which they were worn, as if they were so surely the right thing that once put on they might be safely forgotten altogether, the way in which they brought out every point that would bear inspection, and dexterously subdued those that would not, so that with all Sophy's lack of any real beauty, she was an attractive object, — these were expensive, without doubt. Even the tact and grace with which his hostess, when she found his answers brief and his mind apparently abstracted, passed from the subject which did not seem to interest him, to others more likely to bring him out, and to lead to conversation not so grave as to be depressing, and not so gay as to be out of harmony with whatever secret anxieties he might be feeling, — even the subtly soothing influences of her voice and manner, seemed to him the last crowning achievement of well-spent wealth.

"Without money," he thought, "there is no such thing as living — to call living!" and his money must be won by his own hard work, — the harder, because his self-respect would not allow him to forget what was due to his mother, and what was due to himself in providing for her.

Miss Curtis, as she bade him a kind good-by, gave him the parcel to which she had alluded, — a square flat one, done up with most exquisite nicety, indicating a picture within; and accompanied it with various friendly messages. As he lingered, loath to go, and his eyes upon Sophy while he talked to her cousin, he seemed to take in the whole image of the scene, as a parting sailor does that of his home. He may be away for years; but Arthur was coming back in five days at most; and it was not likely that he should forget, or find when he returned again that anything had changed. The remembrance clung to him through a day of hurried preparation, and hovered like a dream before his half-sleeping, half-waking eyes in the roaring rush of the night train. The chill air of early morning, hanging like gray mist over the dirty old station at Syracuse, dispelled the vision, and he set his face forward to the task of the hour.

The morning train for Liverpool did not leave for some hours; but he had enough to fill up the time. He went to a hotel, took a cup of coffee and a biscuit, and made a very careful and punctilious toilet before he set out again into the principal business street, an unwonted figure at that hour. He paused before a large, thriving-looking shop, whose wares were displayed under the sign "Cubitt and Butler's China Parlors." It was only half-past six, and the front door was closed; but Arthur knew his way to a side door in an alley, and was sure that would be open, and the master within, arranging his stock with the careful but energetic labor of his own hands.

"Hullo, Arthur! that you? Where 'd you drop from?" was his greeting.

"How do you do, John? I came from Boston last night."

"And what's brought you here?" went on the owner of the shop, now hastily wiping his hands on his blue-checked apron, then looking at his visitor's. "Can't shake hands with you, that's a fact; mine ain't clean enough, before breakfast; but I'm glad to see you, whatever you come for." He was shorter than Arthur, but so much more heavily built that he looked the larger man of the two; and the family resemblance between them was so strong that it seemed to emphasize their difference in other respects.

"I came," said Arthur, "because I had a letter from mother, and things seemed in rather a bad way at home. I thought I would stop first and have a talk with you about it, — better here than at your house."

"That's so," said John; "but I don't know as I've much to say."

"If I had supposed, when I bought the house for mother, that the others would come down upon her all at once, I should not have done it. Of course I expect them to visit her, at her own convenience, but she is not strong enough, and she cannot afford, to keep them all the time. Orlando and his family seem to be fixtures."

"Oh, yes, Land," said John, with good-humored contempt in his tone, — "Land will be a fixture, I warrant you. He's got to have some place to roost in, hain't he?"

"He has no right to come down on mother in this way, when he must know perfectly well that her income is not more than sufficient to live comfortably on by herself. And how can she accommodate them? I cannot imagine where she can put them all."

"That's so," said John again, leaning back against his show-case, and folding his arms over his feather-duster; "there's six of them: Land and Ider, three children, — one's a baby to be sure, but it's sick, and I guess it takes up as much room as anybody, — and the girl; to be sure, I guess she pays for *her* board in work."

"And then Jonah."

"Yes, Jone! he counts for one, at any rate, don't he? — a tight squeeze."

"It really ought not to be tolerated."

"Well," said John, "I don't see what you are goin' to do about it."

"I should like to have a better idea how things stand before I go there. What's the matter with Orlando? Can't he get a parish?"

"Oh yes! Land can get a parish; he can get a parish fast enough."

"Cannot keep it — is that it?"

"Oh, yes, he can keep it; they 'd have kep' him at Pompey, if he 'd have stayed."

"Why did he go?"

"Why, the truth of it is, he could n't afford to stay. Preaching pays poorly, you know, unless you can get your name up, and can get a good city parish. We give Dr. Todd three thousand a year. Now, Land preaches and prays very fairly, — I 'll say that for him; but there 's hundreds that do it as well, and he hain't got a mite of push in him. He has to hang round in these country villages, where they give five hundred a year, and they don't give that not half the time, neither; no, he could n't stay at Pompey; they 'd have starved, the whole lot on 'em."

"He ought not to have left one place before he had another in view, at least."

"Well, he had his reasons. The fact was he was in debt, and it was gettin' worse and worse, and he thought he could n't stand it much longer, and that he 'd better get off while he could. What was he to do? — wife always sick, and no end of children."

"He has only three, I believe."

"Only three alive; she 's lost one between the little girl and this last, — born dead; and they ain't been married but five years."

"He had no right to marry under such circumstances."

"I don't see what you 're goin' to do about it," repeated John, coolly.

"If he cannot support his family by the ministry, he ought to go to work at something else."

"Well," said John, as he flicked the dust off a milk-jug on his top shelf, "I hardly know what he 's fit for. It 's a great pity he did n't go in for being a missionary. They 're well looked after, and the children always stand a good chance of being adopted at home; but what 's the use of thinkin' of that now? Ider could n't stand the climate, whatever it might be; and then Land 's too old;

they have to begin young and get up the language, — and the Board would n't take a man of his age, with a family already. I suppose he thinks if he can get a little better call from some other society, perhaps you 'll pay his debts, and let him start free."

"He had better have told me himself than let me hear of it in this way," said Arthur, coldly.

"I think he was sort of shamed to — and then, perhaps, he thought that if he got a place, he might save a little himself; but, Lord bless you! he 'll never do anything at that. Why, they hain't got clothes to wear! It 's a question if Land's got a coat that he could preach in, by this time. It 's a pity, now, that he can't wear your old clothes; you might let him have some; but, good Lord! your pants would be a good two inches up above his ankles, I guess." John waxed voluble as he spoke of the family misfortunes, with a kind of cheerful alacrity, not ill-naturedly, but with some gratification in the idea that he was "taking down Art," whose superior fortunes cost his brother some heart-burnings. Arthur never assumed anything by word or deed; but there was something in his silence, and the fit of his clothes, that was exasperating.

"I must try and make some other arrangement for mother; there is Jonah, — could you find him any place here?"

"I've tried him;" said John, gowing laconic at the least sign of enlargement of the other's speech.

"You did not find it work well?"

"Jone ain't worth his salt, and I don't see why I should keep him on to hurt the business because he's a relation."

"Could not you find some other place for him?"

"I don't want to recommend him to anybody here. The fact is, Jone's lazy as an old hog; you can't shake it out of him. Now, Land will work; yes, I'll say that for him, — Land would work if he only knew how."

"One cannot, and the other will not; it comes to much the same thing."

John shrugged his shoulders. "Seven o'clock," he said, busily stripping off his apron, and the cuffs to match that protected his shirt sleeves, and taking up his coat; "come to breakfast, will you, Art?"

"Thank you, yes; I must take the half-past-eight train for Liverpool."

"And what you goin' to do when you get

there?" asked John, after they had walked a few steps.

"I cannot decide till I do get there."

A few moments more of silence passed, when John, who somehow seemed put more on the defensive by his brother's reticence than by any appeal, direct or indirect, to his feelings, said rather awkwardly, "I'm willing to do what I can for mother. I told her when she left here that she could n't expect me to pay out money for her if she would n't live with me; but I'll give her all her coal, — I can get it with mine, — and I'll see that her house is kept in repair, that is, of course, anything in reason; not while she lets those youngsters of Land's destroy and smash up everything in the way they do. You see, I've got a family of my own to consider; and times are hard."

As he spoke, he opened a gate, and avoiding the front entrance, led the way round a small house covered with boards checked off in squares, and neatly painted in imitation of blocks of gray marble, to a back door opening from a narrow veranda, and they entered the dining-room, where the breakfast-table had been set out over night with what might be termed the stock articles, while Mrs. John

Butler, in the kitchen, labored over the novelties of the season.

"Well, Mr. Butler," she exclaimed, in sharply pitched tones as she came forward, "I hope you've been explainin' to your brother that he mustn't expect anything to speak of in the line of breakfast this morning. I don't calculate to be caught this way, but I haven't got no girl just now, and I ain't accustomed to doin' my own work. Of course," to Arthur, "if I'd known you was comin' I'd have had things different; you'll have to excuse us."

She cast a deprecating look at her stringy dark calico gown, which bore traces of her having "done her own work" for some time past; but the fact that the hair over her forehead was tightly twisted in about a dozen locks round as many hairpins, did not occur to her as anything to mind, for this was the morning uniform of the ladies of her circle; how else could they appear with the tightly frizzled "fringe," the maintenance of which was inexorably demanded as one of their duties to society? A decided mark of her superior position was visible in a pair of diamond earrings, worn all the time, "because it was the safest way."

CHAPTER III.

MRS. JOHN BUTLER was a largely built, loose-jointed woman. Her head was long, especially from the nose downward, and the effect was heightened by all the hair not at present in a preparatory state being tightly strained upward and backward into a knot at the top. She had very black hair and eyes, and a florid complexion, and had an air of being, at least in her own opinion, the superior partner in the household, perhaps because she had been Miss Almira Cubitt, and brought as her dowry, half in the present, and half in the future, the good-will and stock in trade of the China Parlors. She had brought nothing else, — old Cubitt having been content to jog on all his life just holding his business together, till John Butler, with fresher notions and more energy, had used the standpoint of the place and name so as to double the profits in a year or two. John, as well as Arthur, had inherited ambition from their father, — an aspiring young carpenter, who died after a long illness before he had achieved his great aim of becoming a master-builder; and if the elder brother's hopes were more humble, they ran more chance of being satisfied. He now vibrated between a wish to show off his prosperous condition, and a fear that if he indulged it too openly Arthur would think he ought to do more for his mother.

"Come, Arthur," he said, "won't you sit down? We seem to have got rather a picked-up breakfast, but we won't make a stranger of you."

"Of course," repeated Mrs. John, with a toss of her hairpins, "If I 'd known you were comin' I 'd have had things a little different. I 've been lookin' for a girl, but it 's dreadful hard to get them here. Now, Laurea, stop teasin' a bit," — to her five-year-old daughter, who was muttering something in a whining undertone, as she hung on the back of her mother's chair; " 't ain't likely your uncle 's got any candy in his pocket for you."

"I am sorry if your little girl is disappointed," said Arthur, too overwhelmingly polite for the occasion. He was not much used to children, and the present specimen was not prepossessing, — being a stout, heavy child, with a large head and bad teeth, and dark straight hair twisted round bits of rags, with a view, like her mother, to future adornment. "I thought children were not allowed to eat candy now."

"My stars! I guess they'll eat it, whether they're allowed or not. Go to your seat, Laurea, there's a dear;" and then in a loud whisper, "momma'll get you some when we go down street this mornin' if you'll be a good girl, and eat your breakfast."

Laurea — this young lady's name had been invented, or rather adapted, by her mother; "I want her to have a new name that no one else has," Mrs. John had said; "and it's very easy to make one, by just putting an *e* on to Laura" — Laurea subsided, and her father uttering a short and evidently stereotyped grace, the meal began. John Butler was not a church member, for he was not without a conscience, and had an idea that the scruples proper to the character might some time or other stand in the way of business; his wife was one, and that kept him *au courant* with religious affairs, with facilities for strengthening the connection in case of illness or financial depression.

How John had contrived, in the few minutes before breakfast, which he spent in the kitchen drawing the cold water, while his wife dished up her sausages and liver, to acquaint her with the reasons for his brother's visit, and to apprise her of more of the latter's plans than he had himself disclosed, was astonishing to Arthur, who could only suppose that there must be a kind of free-masonry or conversational short-hand between married people. Evidently she was, or thought herself to be, thoroughly informed, and in the first lull of talk, after the weather and spring crops and spring markets had received attention, she struck in with, "If you've any wish to board out the old lady, Mr. Butler, I wish you'd let us have her."

"I have not thought of such a thing as yet," said Arthur; "and at any rate I should want my mother to decide for herself."

"Oh, yes! only it seems a shame to be payin' money out of the family, when it might as well stay in."

"I guess," said John, coloring a little, "that if mother wanted to come here we could fix it for her without chargin' board."

"I believe she prefers her own house," said Arthur.

"Well, if she paid, things would be different here," said Mrs. John. "I'd give her the spare room, and let her have a stove in it. I didn't quite feel as if I could do that before."

Arthur was silent, as he turned over his untasted food with his fork. He was vividly recalling a conversation he had half unconsciously overheard one day, when reading in Miss Curtis's library, between herself and her young cousin. "She is a strong, healthy-looking woman," Sophy had said, "and her references are excellent."

"Her appearance and manner are against her," said Miss Curtis; "I could not have a servant who wore her hair in that alarming way,— and then, her voice!"

"But, Cousin Rachel, for the laundress that wouldn't matter so much, would it, if she were a good worker?— you know you need scarcely see or hear her."

"Yes, I should," said Miss Curtis, decisively. "I should hear that voice through any number of doors; and I could not be happy with such a person anywhere in my house."

Arthur seemed to hear Miss Curtis discussing his sister-in-law. He had never seen the objectionable laundress; but a vivid recollection came up, in contrast to Mrs. John Butler, of the quiet, lady-like, low-voiced and light-footed "perfect treasure" who acted as Miss Curtis's own maid. He was recalled to his sense of the present by his hostess.

"As long as you're going down to Liverpool, Mr. Arthur, would you mind takin' a bundle for me — I mean for them?"

"I shall be most happy."

"It's some clothes of Laurea's I thought they might fix over for the little girl; and I guess I'll send the one she's got on, too," looking at her daughter's frock, a plaid of large design and aggressive colors; "she's about got through with it, and I have n't any to make it over with."

"Yes," said John, "let 'em have it, let 'em have it. I'll buy Laurea a new one, — or two, for that matter."

"Ider and her sister will turn up their noses at it; they'll say it's too high colored or somethin' else. They ain't very grateful, and they've got such queer notions. You see they were raised by an aunt of theirs, and *she* was an old maid."

"You knew Mrs. Orlando Butler before her marriage?"

"Law, yes! I should think I did know Ider

Shepherd! They come from New Hampshire to Cazenovia after their father died. I used to visit Uncle Ezra Whitten there, and I went to the Female Academy to take music lessons. Old Miss Shepherd come there to teach, and brought the girls with her. She was a queer old thing, if ever there was one. She brought them girls up to think it was sinful to look at a man. I don't know how Ider ever got married; though she was rather pretty, too, if she ever had any style. She's not so much like her aunt as Florer is."

Arthur excused himself for hurrying away by pleading the necessity of catching his train, and was permitted to depart, carrying with him a large parcel, particularly ill done up in newspaper, while John warmly urged him to come again whenever he could, and Mrs. John vainly tried to make Laurea send her love to her little cousins. "The fact is," said her mother, "them children are such young scamps that Laurea don't take no comfort in 'em."

Arthur walked off, unpleasantly conscious of the conspicuous appearance he made in carrying a large bundle of the young lady's out-grown clothes; but when he entered the stuffy car in the "way train," which passed twice a day through Liverpool, he found that parcels of all kinds were the rule among the passengers, and that his own would pass unnoticed. He sat by the window, looking out at the well-remembered scenes along the road, but little changed since he had gone over it when a boy, though then a ride on the train had been a rare treat, and more often he had trudged the five miles and back. How long the way had been then, and how short it seemed now!

There was the budding veil of creepers, hiding with their tender green the banks of every railway cutting; for Onondaga soil is rich, and Nature takes upon herself the unpaid task, but for her left undone, of beautifying the surroundings of the New York Central Railroad and its branches. There was Onondaga Lake, shallow and with flat shores, yet giving the air of freshness and freedom that only water can give to a landscape. Liverpool, on the bank, was not without its natural advantages, but it had an air, like a pretty woman with slovenly habits, of not making the best of itself. It was built round a great open green, where the now budding elms threw their branches so high into the air as to let the light in beneath to color the springing grass; but the place was unkempt and untrimmed, and spring, here, was a less becoming period of the year than it ought to have been, as the inhabitants, who acted with deliberation, had not yet taken time to remove the piles of ashes and rubbish which had accumulated in their yards during winter. The view of the lake was cut off by the long rows of salt-sheds which lined the shore. They were empty now, the business having forsaken Liverpool for more productive fields, and they were not objects to look picturesque in decay.

Arthur stopped at the inn, or rather boarding-house, wrote some business letters, and leaving his luggage there walked across the green, all very quiet and still in the soft sweet air, to a little frame-house, the home of his mother's early married life, built, and well-built, though in the worst style of a period of ugly houses, by her husband's own hands. When he found she could not be happy at his brother's he had paid off the mortgage on it, and had it thoroughly put in order for her; but it now seemed to have relapsed into the state in which he remembered it in his boyhood, when they had not a penny to spare for repairs. The fence was broken here and there, and looked like the one he used so painfully to try to patch up to keep the neighbors' hens from scratching in the small plot of ground where he strove to raise a few vegetables. The shrubs which he had so recently ordered for the little garden were some uprooted and dying, some crushed and broken; flower-borders and grass-plats alike were trodden hard and bare; and a cinder-heap in the back-ground was full in view.

"Disgusting!" he thought to himself, as he strode up the path; it was not uttered aloud, for he seldom allowed himself to show outward signs of disturbance; but a sharp and sudden knock against his ankle drew one of an emphatic nature from him. It came, as he now saw, from a stone thrown by a child about four years old, while a younger one launched a broken door-handle with equal ill-will, but less dexterity. These young persons were indistinguishable as to sex, both being clad from head to foot in long brown pinafores, over which hung long fair curling hair, which streamed in the wind as they now fled wildly round the corner of the house, from their favorite playing-place, the cinder-heap, only pausing to throw back grimaces over their shoulders as they disappeared. If these were the cousins to whose manners Miss Laurea objected, it must be owned that she had some excuse; but the little savages were so very pretty that even in spite of the unpleasant tingling sensation in his ankle, Arthur felt inclined to take their part against her.

He advanced and turned a handle in the middle of the door, which struck a bell on the inside, apparently more adapted to be heard by the visitor's own ears than by those of any inhabitant. For some moments no one came, and he had time to contemplate the battered door and broken doorscraper, with a fresh emotion of anger, which vented itself in a more violent turn of the crank. His perturbation made his usually attentive ear miss the sound of a light step within, and as the door swung open, he started back with feelings akin to those which might have been experienced by that familiar heroine of the nursery, Mrs. Bond, if when seeking in her pond for the familiar domestic fowl of the ditty, a splendid white swan had swelled its plumage full in her face. The most beautiful girl he had ever seen in his life was looking at him, her eyes almost on a level with his. There was something, too, in the backward set of her lovely shoulders, and her cool dazzling fairness that could have maintained the comparison.

"I beg your pardon!" he involuntarily exclaimed; "I thought no one had heard me ring."

"I could not come at first," said the girl, with no apologetic accent, but as if stating a fact.

"Is Mrs. Butler at home?"

"She is," said the beauty, moving slightly aside to let him pass into the little front sitting-room.

"Will you be so good as to let her know that Mr. Arthur Butler wishes to see her? I believe," he went on, "I have the pleasure of speaking to Miss —" He had actually forgotten in his confusion the maiden name of his brother Orlando's wife, whose sister, he supposed, must now be standing before him.

"I am Flora," said the girl, coldly, and without a smile; but her words resolved the puzzling effort to find a resemblance in her face, which he now recognized as being to his favorite statue, her namesake at the Capitol, though he knew only by photographs that image of divine girlhood, so sweetly and fitly crowned with a wreath of roses. This poor little goddess had lost her wreath in the rough ways of life, but the few curving lines which defined the soft contours of her youthful face were the same; the same, those exquisite beauties he had most especially admired: the firm but fine-drawn outlines of the mouth; the chin so lightly set upon, yet so gently melting into the round slender throat; and the soft texture of the skin on the temples at the roots of the backward rippling hair, as if faintly powdered with gold-dust, which showed even in the pictured marble. She was paler than one would have imagined her prototype, but no sculptured goddess ever made one imagine such eyes, — long in shape, with a thick, dark fringe, and a languishing curve and droop, that might have suggested coquetry, but that there was no sparkle in their blue depths, nothing but pure color full of latent light, like the sky. She wore a very limp, faded, chocolate-brown calico gown, one of Mrs. John Butler's cast-off dresses, but it seemed designed for as perfect a foil to her fairness as the withered spathe that clings to the open blossom of a white narcissus.

Arthur took all this in half consciously,

while she opened the parlor window and the closed blinds, and then saying, "I will tell Mrs. Butler you are here," floated off, leaving him to inhale a fragrance compounded of the scent of old boots, muddy carpets, carbolic acid, and last week's dinners, carefully preserved like pot-pourri, by keeping it shut up. In a few moments Mrs. Butler, a small, delicate, still pretty woman, who looked a lady in her severely plain, cheap black gown, worn as much from principle as economy, hurried in and greeted her son affectionately, though in a pre-occupied way.

"You must excuse a very poor dinner, Arthur, my dear," she began, with a nervous and deprecating air, as of one who expects to be found fault with; "we did not expect you till the afternoon train."

"That is of no consequence."

"I have been trying to think where you are to sleep, but we are so full — perhaps we can arrange a bed in this room."

"You must not trouble yourself. I have engaged a room at Kemp's, and I can take my meals there too, if it will save you trouble."

"Oh, no, of course we want to have you eat here — if you don't mind; you won't expect much when there's sickness in the house." Mrs. Butler, as she spoke, fidgeted restlessly about, and changed her seat once or twice. Her son felt that it was cruel that he should be such an object of alarm, and though he had included her in some of the indignation he had expressed, he realized, as he always did when he was with her, that she was scarcely to blame. "She's not fit to take care of herself," he thought.

"Dinner is ready," said Flora, appearing again, and each time a fresh surprise, at the door, but vanishing so quickly that by the time they reached the next room she had left it. The small apartment was already well filled by Arthur's younger brothers; for though the inheritance of the father's energy had apparently been exhausted by his two eldest sons, the younger approached him more nearly in size. The Rev. Orlando Butler, like his maternal grandfather a clergyman of the Presbyterian Church, was a tall thin loose-built man, with sloping shoulders; and his long close-shaven face, and near-sighted eyes, above which the hair was already growing thin on the top of his head, had a gentle, deprecating expression, just now more marked than usual. He wore a faded old wrapper, and old slippers down at the heel, but there was a certain look of refinement in spite of it all, which gave his outward presence something akin to his brother Arthur's fastidious elegance. His attention was vehemently claimed by his children, one of whom had hold of each hand, and who made such pertinacious resistance to letting go, that he was obliged to give up the attempt to shake hands with their uncle. They were now very neatly dressed in frocks of butcher-blue linen, with the proper distinction in masculine and feminine cut and make, and their rich golden hair, combed out into a glittering wavy mane, made them look elaborately attired.

Jonah Butler, who rose with a yawn from an old sofa where he had been lounging, was as tall as Orlando, and twice as broad, — a great hulking vegetable-looking lout, who needed pruning. As they sat down Flora came in for a moment, flushed and hurried, with her dress unchanged, and carrying a large tray, which, still holding, she deftly loaded with a selection from the dishes on the table. Still balancing the heavy weight on her left hand, she tried to open the door with the other, when Arthur sprang up, and taking it from her before she could refuse, opened it himself.

"Thank you," she murmured, in the lowest tone, and for the first time with some recognition in her eyes.

"Where can I take it for you, Miss Shepherd?"

"Thank you, I must take it myself; it is Ida's dinner," she said rather earnestly, as if she expected him to insist on retaining it; but he gave it up at once as soon as he saw that she really wished it, and she disappeared immediately.

"Is Flora coming to dinner?" asked Mrs. Butler.

"No," said Orlando; "the baby is awake, and she will have to hold him while Ida has hers."

"It is a pity the baby will always wake at meal times," said Mrs. Butler; "it takes away Ida's appetite to hear it cry."

Indeed, through the open door a wail was now heard, repeated at regular intervals, like the mewing of a sickly kitten, though each individual cry was so feeble that it seemed as if it must be the last. It was not so much like a complaint occasioned by any particular discomfort, as a protest against the misery of living altogether; but after a while it suddenly ceased, and the equally faint but more steady sound of a half-murmured lullaby came with more or less distinctness, as if the singer were moving about.

"It is a great mistake to walk with babies to stop their crying," said Mrs. Butler; "I never did with any of you."

"Ida must have her dinner in peace," said Orlando, with a sigh; "she eats little enough." He did not himself make much show of appetite, but spent most of his time cutting up his children's meat, coaxing them to eat a little, and allowing them to waste a great deal, for they had capricious appetites to match their dainty looks. Jonah, on the contrary, devoured in silence about a pound of corned-beef, with accompaniments in like measure. Neither spectacle was conducive to Arthur's enjoyment of the occasion, and indeed the dinner, though cooked by the fair hands of the beautiful Flora, was, it must be confessed, a very uninviting repast. As soon as it was over, without much having been said by any one, Orlando took the children upstairs, where their aunt took off their blue frocks, the only respectable garments they possessed, and in which it was her intention to produce them again at tea, and put on the discarded calico aprons.

"Who's that man?" asked Orlando the second.

"Your uncle Arthur, my dear."

"I don't like him, then," said the boy, pouting like a sulky Cupid.

"I did frow stones at man," lisped the girl, smiling like a cherub in bliss.

"And I hit him," added her brother, with more distinct speech.

"Oh, children, children! you will break my heart!" cried the aunt, in despair. The truth was that all her calculations had been wofully upset. Mrs. Butler had been sure that dear Arthur would want to spend the day with dear John, and would not arrive in Liverpool till evening, by which time Flora had hoped to make the children presentable. She had carefully cut their silken hair straight across their brows, where it lay in such light wavy fringes, and cast such pearly shadows on their translucent skins, that it seemed an insult when Mrs. Almira took up the style and "banged," as she called it, Laurea's thick dark coarse straight locks like a dead wall just over her eyebrows.

Then Flora had done up their blue frocks as nicely as she could, feeling that if Ida herself could not appear, the sight of her children might be enough to melt the hard heart of the uncle, whom the family idea depicted as rolling in money, and able to do a great deal more for them than he did, if he only wanted to. Hot tears rose to her eyes, as she led the little reprobates downstairs, and lured them with some hoarded bits of broken crockery to confine their afternoon sports to the rubbish-heap by the back door; while she went in to clear off the table, relieved to find that the dining-room was deserted, and that she could pick her own cold dinner from among the scraps left, without being stared at by Jonah from the lounge. Arthur, as soon as dinner was over, had said to his younger brother:—

"Will you go to Kemp's and ask for a couple of parcels I left there? Some things Almira sent, and a little present I brought for you," he added in explanation to his mother.

"O—h—h— too heavy for you, hey?" drawled Jonah, with an effort at sarcasm.

"You seem to have nothing to do, so you may as well go."

"Too grand to carry a bundle yourself, be yer?" inquired Jonah, with as much of a sneer as his heavy features could give; but he rose all the same. He never disobeyed Arthur to his face.

Mrs. Butler knew that her son wanted to improve the opportunity for a *tête-à-tête* with her, which she dreaded, and thought it well to put off by murmuring something about "helping Flora clear off;" so she lingered in the dining-room, scraping the leavings from one plate into another, as if with some vague idea that they would disappear in the process, and putting away all the clean dishes into the wrong places. When Flora had at last set everything to rights in a way which left nothing for her to do, she finally changed her apron with trembling hands, and went into the parlor, hoping that Orlando would come down to speak for himself; but he did not.

CHAPTER IV.

"I AM very sorry to find things in such a condition here," began Arthur with his usual polish of manner, as if he were addressing a stranger, but which was more alarming to his mother than if he had flown out at her in a rage; "the boys ought to have known better than to come down upon you in this way."

"I am very sorry," murmured Mrs. Butler.

"May I ask what Orlando's plans are — if he has any?"

"I hope Orlando will soon get some good parish."

"Has he any in view?"

"I do not think he has; but you know a minister has to wait for a call."

"He has been waiting six months, it seems, and living on you in the mean time. I don't suppose that what I have sent you has been enough to support such a family, and I want to know if you owe anything here, and how much."

"I am afraid we do — but I can't exactly say; I hope it is not very much."

"Who does know?"

"I suppose the storekeeper will have it on his books, will he not? He will show them to you, if you ask."

"And can you tell me if his books are correct?"

"Oh, they must be! Mr. Taylor is a professing Christian! Perhaps, Arthur, you might pay him a little while you are here, and I think he would wait for the rest."

"Till when?"

"I don't know — till Orlando gets a parish, I suppose."

"It seems he could not pay his own bills when he had a parish."

"He has had a great deal of sickness in his family, you know; but Orlando has a great feeling against being in debt; he gave up his parish at Pompey because he thought it was not a good example for a minister to set."

"Does he think that it is a good example for a minister to set to come and make his mother run in debt by living upon her?"

"It would be hard if he could not expect his mother to help him;" said Mrs. Butler, in a trembling voice.

"If you could, — but you have not the means; and he knew that perfectly well when he came here."

"I suppose," said Mrs. Butler, tearfully, "that he thought —"

"That I should pay them for him? Very likely."

"I should think you would feel it a credit to have a minister in the family, and want to do a little something for him."

"I cannot consider such conduct a credit to any one, minister or no minister. The fact is, that I have always done all I could for you, and more than all the others put together; and though I have had to economize closely, I never ran into debt. I have done something for the boys, too. I gave John and Orlando presents when they were married, the best I could afford, and I kept Jonah at school, till I found he was learning nothing. I say these things, not to boast, but to show that they have no right to expect more of me."

"I hope Jonah will soon find something to do; and we really have needed him at home this winter; he goes all our errands to the store."

"I cannot afford to pay him for doing that."

"I wish," said Mrs. Butler, now melting into tears, "that some one would give us some money. Perhaps the Ladies' Home Missionary Society — they gave Orlando his education, you know — would help us a little."

Arthur Butler was sorry for his mother, and felt as uncomfortable as a man usually does at the sight of a woman's tears; but he had no deeper feeling, never having had any sympathy with either of his parents, or any special affection for them, except that languid one of habit. He had just enough of his mother's personal refinement to make him, as a child, repelled by his father's coarse, overbearing ways; and enough of his father's energy to be provoked at his mother's fatuity; while having twice the brains of either of them, his sense of these qualities was less likely to be deadened by custom. Indeed, Mrs. Butler herself could hardly have been said to love the husband, whom she had married because he asked, or rather told her to do so; and had he lived longer, perhaps his love would have died out as the pretty face faded by which it had been won.

It was useless, Arthur felt, to say any

more to her now on this theme; he realized for the hundredth time the impossibility of making her understand; and after standing a few moments looking blankly out of the window, he asked abruptly: "Where did — Orlando's wife come from?"

"It is a very romantic story," said Mrs. Butler, glad to change the subject, and always mildly interested in anything "like a story," as she called it; and she proceeded in the style of the tales in the "Lady's Book" which she had read in her giddy youth, before her conversion, since which period she had touched no work of fiction. "Ida and Flora were two lovely orphans, born and brought up in a beautiful but secluded valley in New Hampshire, where their father, a poor but pious clergyman —"

"I thought you said they were orphans."

"Oh, that was not till afterwards. Their father died more than five years ago, when Ida was seventeen, and Flora fourteen. Their mother had long been dead, and their aunt, a maiden lady, but a very remarkable woman, had kept house for their father, and brought them up. She had taught in a very fine school in Boston, and when Mr. Shepherd died, she got a situation as assistant principal in the Female Seminary in Cazenovia, where Orlando had just been settled. Orlando thought a great deal of Miss Esther Shepherd; and she thought a great deal of him. He always said she was as fine an example of female piety as he ever saw."

"Where is she now?"

"In a better world," said Mrs. Butler. "She passed away three years ago, just about the time Flossy was born."

Arthur would have asked more, but Jonah appeared at the door, and Mrs. Butler had only time to say, pleadingly, "She was sick a great while, and most of her savings were used up; but Ida and Flora have each a nice little income of thirty dollars of their own; and it saves a girl for us to have Flora, — she is very smart."

"Here they be," grunted Jonah, dumping the parcels he carried on to the hair-cloth sofa, from which they rolled, and had to be picked up again. Mrs. Butler opened the larger one with some curiosity, and said that Almira was always so kind and liberal, but her taste was too gay for her, and she wished the things were a little plainer, more suitable for a minister's family; but it was very good in her to remember them. She was still turning over the contents, crumpled from close packing, when Flora appeared in the doorway with the usual quiet which characterized her movements. In her arms she carried the baby, which for a wonder happened to be awake and silent; and which she hoped, might produce a favorable impression on the uncle, and perhaps do something toward effacing that so unfortunately made by its brother and sister. The baby was very thin and small, but it had a sweet little face, and at any rate it could not throw stones; so she put on its best frock, and wrapped it in a white shawl which had been her mother's. That it might be the better set off, she wore her own best gown, an old blue cashmere, faded, but of a pretty shade, and the only one she possessed which had really been made for her; but that was a long time ago, and it would not meet in front, so she turned it away at the neck, threw an old muslin handkerchief over her shoulders, and knotting it loosely in front, thought that on the whole it looked very well.

"Here is your dear little namesake, Arthur," said Mrs. Butler; "I suppose you were very much pleased to be remembered, were you not?"

Flora looked at the baby, and then shyly at Arthur, as if to claim his attention for it; but his eyes were fixed on her. No man had ever looked at her in such a way before. She had never had a lover who had passed beyond the first stage of courtship; and that stage was only associated in her mind with forward remarks, and rude attempts at gallantry, which had frightened her and made her shrink away, and cling for protection even to the yet more timid Ida.

As she stood with the baby in her arms, its weight too light to give any impression of effort in the holding, and yet enough to give balance and poise to the long graceful lines of her figure, Arthur was thinking that she made a lovelier image than had yet been given to the world of that blended expression which should mark the Virgin Mother. He was too penetrated with her presence to think that he was a young man looking at a girl, till he saw her dazzling fairness flush with a rosy glow like a snowpeak in the sunrise; and then he turned away, feeling that if he looked longer now, the worship might profane the shrine. He wondered if Ida were half as beautiful as her sister, and thought that if she were, it was an act of great presumption in Orlando to have married her; and then he wished, as he always did when he saw anything lovely in nature or art, that he could share his pleasure with Miss Curtis. How she would enjoy it! As for him, it was well, he thought, that he could look on beauty with a purely artistic delight of the eye alone.

"It is very small, is it not?" he asked, trying to pay due attention to the baby; "it is odd to think that they can be so tiny."

"It is improving, we hope," said Mrs. Butler, "since we put it on 'Mellin's food;' the only trouble is that it is very expensive."

Arthur did not feel competent to discuss the subject, and took up the other parcel, saying, "I have brought a little present for you, mother, from a friend of mine — Miss Curtis."

"Courtin', be yer?" asked Jonah, with a more knowing grin than usual; and Mrs. Butler looked anxious as she said, "I hope she is a nice young lady, I am sure, for your sake, Arthur. Is she a professor of religion? How long have you known her?"

"For several years," said Arthur; "but there is nothing of what you imagine. Miss Curtis, I should think, must be as old as you." He looked at his mother a little doubtfully. She had been a very pretty little woman, and was still a very pretty little old lady, but to think of her as a contemporary of Miss Curtis seemed thoroughly absurd.

"Is she a Christian?" went on Mrs. Butler.

"Certainly."

"And what denomination does she belong to?"

"She is a member of Trinity Church."

"Oh, an Episcopalian," said Mrs. Butler, with a slight shade of disappointment. "Still, my dear, Episcopalians may be Christians; I have known several excellent ones in that denomination;" and she slowly drew from the parcel, which Arthur had untied, a colored group of angels, after Fra Angelico.

"Ah, yes; it is very pretty, and it seems a sacred subject; did the lady paint it herself, my dear?"

"No, it is a chromo-lithograph. Miss Curtis has been very kind to me, mother, and she sent you her regards, and thought you might enjoy the picture, as it is a favorite of her own."

"She is very kind, I am sure. How did

you come to know her? Did she board in the same house with you?"

"No, I met her in society, and she has invited me a great deal."

"Does she live with friends?"

"No; in her own house."

"Has she a house of her own? I suppose she is well off."

"Yes."

"Perhaps," said Mrs. Butler, "she might do something for us, if you asked her. Couldn't you tell her all about us, — Orlando's being a minister, and Ida's having such poor health? She might feel disposed to help us."

"I could not possibly ask her."

"I wish I knew her, and I bet you I'd ask her," said Jonah.

"I don't see why not," said his mother. "I remember my dear father had a rich and pious friend, Mr. Isaac Jacobus, of Utica, who used to send him all his old clothes; they fitted exactly, and he seldom had to buy any. I dare say Miss Curtis would gladly take up a collection among her friends for us."

Arthur said no more; but there was something in his silence that made Flora glad to seize a chance to carry the baby off; it was falling asleep, and must be laid down. It was always going to sleep, but it never stayed asleep long, — its feeble vitality perpetually calling for food, which only satisfied it for a few moments. She put it down, however, and stood looking at it for a breathing-space, while the flush faded from her face. She had been prepared to dislike Arthur Butler by his letter, which his mother had shown her, — Mrs. Butler was one of those women who show every letter they receive to everybody in the house, — but he did not seem like the man who had written it, or, what she had imagined him, something like his brother John, only better educated. Mrs. Butler was always fearing that her two oldest sons were growing "worldly and fashionable;" but Arthur, if he resembled any one she had ever seen before, reminded her of her own father, to whom those words certainly did not apply. Nay, there was even something about his elegant attire and the way he wore it that recalled the country minister's old coats and hats. The softened tone to women, the courtesies unobtrusively offered, the gentle deference, as to beings set apart, which had never been wanting from "Parson Shepherd" to any woman, even to his little school-girl daughters, had made him, in the estimation of his female parishioners, "a real gentleman." That they could exist in a young man, and a man of the world, was a revelation; a revelation, too, the admiration for her beauty that gave them a more personal application. Orlando was kind and good, and indulgent to feminine weaknesses; but his religion had taught him that "favor was deceitful, and beauty was vain;" and even his seventeen-year-old bride, in the budding bloom of her youth, had never moved him to love's foolish ecstasies.

It was a mercy for Flora that she had no more time to think over these problems; the few minutes she had were too much. She was soon busy again, and did not appear at tea, except to fill her sister's tray; and she stayed up stairs to put the children to bed, and settle Ida for the night, while Orlando, enveloped in a big apron, patiently toiled to clear away below, and Mrs. Butler, in the sitting-room, told Arthur that Flora was a remarkable girl, and could do anything. Her father had fitted her to teach before his death, and she was a splendid sick-nurse; she had nursed her aunt for two years with a cancer, and had taken care of Ida since the baby was three days old.

Arthur did not come to breakfast the next morning, thinking that his presence at so early an hour might be an incumbrance in the small, crowded house. He went out to walk, and think over the hopeless muddle of family affairs, and in the midst of his thinking came upon Orlando, coming from the village store; for though this was the one piece of domestic duty at which Jonah never rebelled, he had not of late been as useful in it as formerly, the store-keeper beginning to find that he was suddenly out of the articles required. Orlando, in his clerical character, could still command respect and attention, and though it was unpleasant for him to ask for what he might never be able to pay for, what can a husband and father do when his sickly baby refuses to eat anything but Mellin's Food? He had found the people unusually civil to-day, owing to rumors of Arthur's arrival in the town, and was returning with his little parcel in his hand when the brothers met. They could not talk over their private affairs in the street, empty as it was; but when they had reached home and crossed the little garden, where Jonah, also under the influence of that overmastering presence, had begun to spade up the ground in an aimless way, and walked round to the back door of the house, Arthur threw himself on the bench in the porch, with "I should like to have a few words with you, Orlando."

"In a moment," said Orlando, entering the house with his parcel; and under the circumstances perhaps he cannot be blamed if the moment extended to two, which gave Arthur, always self-possessed, time to get his breath and muster his thoughts, and he began with alarming formality:—

"You know that I have supported my mother almost entirely since I was fifteen, though not at first as well as I could wish. Of late years I have been able to give her a sum large enough to keep her in comfort, — quite as large as, with her simple habits, she required. I was obliged for years to practise the greatest economy to do this. I never expected any of my brothers to help me. Such little assistance as John chooses to give I never asked, though I am willing for his own sake to accept it. I offer no complaint, and I make no boast. I should have felt it beneath me to do any less. Now I find that you have all come down upon her, and are eating up her substance. The allowance I make her is certainly not enough to keep such a family. What reason have you to suppose that I am able, even if inclined, to give any more?"

"I don't know," said Orlando, dejectedly, — "I did not like to bring the whole family to mother's, but it seemed the best, that is, the only thing to do under the circumstances; and I did not think that it would last so long."

"How much longer do you suppose it will last?"

"I cannot say. Dr. Griscom hopes that if Ida goes on as well as she is doing now, she can come downstairs in another week or two. It all depends upon the baby; worrying about him keeps her back terribly. I may be able to get off and preach somewhere as a candidate. I should have gone before, but I really could not leave her."

"I am sorry for your difficulties, but I don't see that they give you the right to deprive my mother, for whom you have never done anything, of the comforts of her home, and what is worse, of her reputation. John tells me you have left your parish in debt. It seems to me that it would have been better to stay and face it out than to come here and start afresh upon her credit."

"I hoped when I came to find something to do."

"The church here is empty, it seems. Was there any chance of their giving you a call?"

"No," said Orlando, with a little reluctance; "I — I don't think that a man has much chance of a call where he was born and brought up. I thought I should get the weddings and funerals and such; but it has unfortunately happened that they have generally come when I was unable to attend them."

"You can hardly expect people to time their exit from the world so as to put burial-fees into your pocket," said Arthur. Orlando made no answer, and his brother went on: "I suppose you thought you had something to fall back upon. You knew me well enough to feel sure that I would never allow my mother to be in debt in my native town. Wringing money out of me in this way may accord with the character of a clergyman;

I cannot say that it does with my notion of a gentleman."

"I did think you might be willing to do a little for us."

"My being willing, as I have told you before, is not the point; you had no reason to know that I was able. You know that I earned every cent that I paid for my own education, and that while I was helping my mother, even from the first, I had no assistance till I won a scholarship at college; while you were educated by the Ladies' Home Missionary Society, and kept into the bargain. You are only a year younger than I am, and the start they gave you ought to have counterbalanced that. I made one resolution which I have never broken, that I would never get into debt. What I spent, I earned first. If I had to run in debt now to pay what you owe here, I would not do it; but do it I shall, and that before I leave this place."

"I hope it is not going to be too great an inconvenience to you."

"Your anxiety comes rather late. I have asked Taylor to send his account in to me to-night. Are there any others?"

"There is Mr. Snyder for milk, and the

butcher for meat and vegetables, — but that is not much."

"Get them for me this afternoon, if you please. Have you any doctor's bill?"

"Oh, no, Dr. Griscom never charges me anything. He would not to a minister's family."

"I do not see why he should give his time for nothing to them, any more than they should to him. Does he pay no pew-rent?"

"He never goes to meeting, you know;" said Orlando, simply.

"I presume," said Arthur, "if he doctors the clergy for nothing, he must see enough of them elsewhere."

Orlando made no answer to this sarcasm, and Arthur, angry at having lowered himself by making it, was silent too for a moment, and then began again, still in the same slow, serene, exquisitely modulated voice: "The fact is, Orlando, you began wrong. Your trade, if you will excuse me for saying so, is a beggarly one, unless you can stand at the top of it. First, your education was given you, and you were supported while you had it, out of a parcel of old women's money-boxes; that takes the stuff out of a man, and makes him go on passing the hat round the rest of his life. Our grandfather was always doing so, and mother was brought up to think it a matter of course. I suppose your father-in-law brought up his family on the same principle; it is the badge of the tribe. Now, if the supply is greater than the demand in this business, or if you don't know how to meet the demand, I should say you had better try something else."

"I am sure," said Orlando, in a trembling voice, "I would gladly do anything I could for the support of my wife and children. I did hope — I hope I have not been altogether useless in the ministry, but I know that he that provideth not for his own is worse than a heathen."

"I should feel more disposed to help you if you had been more ingenuous with me from the first, and asked for help, instead of screwing it out of me in this way; I suppose you must stay on here till you find something, but you must keep a strict account of your expenses here, and forward it to me weekly. Your debts in Pompey you cannot expect me to take up."

"Thank you," said Orlando; "we will try

to be as saving as we can. You are very kind."

It was now Arthur's turn to feel as if his brother might be indulging in satire, though nothing could be less meaning than the tone in which these words were said, and he answered, with the first sign of irritation he had shown: "There is one way in which I should like to see you saving less; you seem to be getting all the household work out of that girl, and letting her pay you for doing it; it strikes me that the bargain is a dear one at thirty dollars a year."

Orlando, who had winced somewhat under his brother's previous sarcasms, looked surprised at this one, as if the idea were entirely new to him. "Flora would not be happy away from Ida," he quietly remarked; "she would not go if I should try to make her."

"It is scandalous," said Arthur, with rising heat; "you ought to have one servant, at least, to relieve her. See that you get one as soon as possible, and I will pay her wages."

"Well," said Orlando, — "if you can afford so much money. Girls are very hard to get here, and indeed I hardly know where we can put one now, the house is so full."

"Get one to come by the day, then."

"That would cost a great deal more."

"Never mind how much it costs. I will not have a young lady cooking my dinner when I come here. It is not proper work for her."

"Almost all our ladies here do their own work," said Orlando, still mildly astonished. "Even John's wife does, a good deal of the time."

Arthur reddened, conscious that there was something silly and snobbish in the tone of his last remark, coming from a man who had so many times seen his mother over the cooking-stove or washing-tub; conscious too, that if Flora had been Mrs. John's sister, and cut out on her pattern, the spectacle of her doing any kind of work would have been one to regard with equanimity. He felt that he was put at a disadvantage in continuing the discussion and was glad when a somewhat awkward pause was broken by the ringing of the bell for dinner, at which meal Flora appeared with burning cheeks, the heat produced by cooking on a languid spring day having been doubled by overhearing the whole of the above conversation, carried on in audible masculine tones just outside the kitchen window, at a point where running away meant ruin to a not over abundant repast. She had the uncomfortable sensation, doubly so to a woman, of not being able thoroughly to take part with either speaker. She thought Arthur hard and cruel, and yet she could not but own that what he said had some justice in it. She loathed, herself, to be in debt, and she thought of her father's and her aunt Esther's housekeeping, where every penny due was paid before Saturday night; but then no one was ever ill, or lazy, in those far-off, far-away, halcyon days!

As to what was said of herself, personally, it touched her little. They had never kept a servant at her father's, and Aunt Esther had always said household work was a fit and proper occupation for a lady, and that all the noble women in history and poetry were proficients in it. Only, Aunt Esther's housekeeping was in a different style from this, — a housekeeping of white curtains and flowers in the windows, and dainty little dishes and old china on the table. She had not time to do anything now as it ought to be done, and she knew that every day she was giving up something that her aunt had thought essential. But let things be as bad as they would, she would never have a servant to help her whose wages were to come out of Mr. Arthur Butler's pocket!

CHAPTER V.

"ARTHUR'S going to take me to ride this afternoon;" said Mrs. Butler, as they rose from the table. "I asked if he would n't get Hazard's double team, and then you could come too, Orlando, and take the children."

"Flora must go;" said Orlando.

"Thank you very much, but I cannot possibly," said Flora, as she left the room.

"I don't see how she can leave," said Mrs. Butler.

Arthur said nothing, agreeable as the prospect of the exchange was; but Orlando, leaving the room in his turn, pursued his sister-in-law into the depths of the kitchen: "Come, Flora, you must go; it will do you good."

"You are very kind, Orlando, but I don't see how I can. If you will go, and take Landy and Flossy, it will be the best thing you can do; I can get plenty of time then for all the work."

"So can I," said Orlando; and seeing that she looked doubtful of his powers, he cut short the argument by saying, "Come, come, child! run along! you must get out sometimes, and you will work better when you come home. I insist upon it," he added. There was a little touch of decision about him when he spoke to his wife and her sister, and Flora turned slowly away. She did not know whether she wanted most to go or to stay at home; but when she had hastily dressed herself and run downstairs, her heart was beating fast with that tumultuous pleasure that presages pain, — perhaps because, at nineteen, it was years since she had had any pleasure properly so-called. Arthur was waiting at the door, having already settled his mother carefully on the back seat of the wagon, with Flossy by her side.

As the two children, for the sake of peace, could not be trusted together, Master Orlando must sit in front, between his uncle and aunt, — "like a family" as Jonah remarked from the doorstep, rather provoked that he had not been asked when there was plenty of room. But his words fell unheeded on the ears of the pair as they drove away from indoor cares and darkness in the quivering light air of early spring, — too soft, too sweet, too new to make one feel the need of more shade than was given by the tender budding boughs. Arthur drove a lively pair of bay horses, and drove them well. He had had no early training in this and kindred pursuits; but he knew that they were part of a gentleman's education; he had not in college worked harder at his books than at athletics of all kinds, trying to replace the second nature of early habit by the putting of a powerful mind to master every minute detail; and he had succeeded so far that he now seemed to throw no effort into his easy handling of the reins, and had plenty of attention to spare for his fair companion. She wore her blue cashmere dress and white fichu, and on the back of her head, the only place where it would fit, a large, old, broad-brimmed, black straw hat, too rusty and broken for even Orlando's wear; but she had covered it with coarse black net fulled on and drawn into a great rosette at one side. Even set sharply against this background, the lines of her throat and chin were too soft, too delicate, to be fitly shown by the finest pencil line, and every crisp bright tendril of her hair shone separate out in a way no brush could imitate. They were close before his eyes, and the arm that she had thrown round the little boy was so near that her small ungloved hand touched his coat. Flora had no gloves or sunshade, and no money to buy them; but as she faced the sun for a ten-mile drive, the pearly whiteness of her skin seemed intensified by the light, while the heightened color on her cheek looked like some transient effect of cloud or rainbow, too bright to last. "Really," he thought, "she has enough points to fit out a dozen professional beauties. Why, her very hair is enough to found a reputation on!" His being able to notice all these attractions so minutely and accurately showed that there was no danger, any more than there might be from a picture he might admire, and made him feel safe in trying to penetrate a little below the surface.

"Have you been on many of the drives about here?" he began as they bowled smoothly along.

"I have not been on any."

"Then I will choose one, if you don't mind. The country here has not much to boast of; it is rather out of the way of the scenery districts of New York; but it is rich and fertile, and fields and farms anywhere look pleasant in spring."

"It is pretty," said Flora, shyly, "very pretty, but it seems to want something; I don't know how to express it, but it is all so much alike."

"It wants what a painter would call composition, you mean? That is the lack in a great deal of our pretty rural scenery; this rolling ground with one great swelling field after another, lacks point and contrast."

"There are beautiful trees here though," said Flora, looking admiringly at a row of tall oaks in a hedgerow. "I wish there were more of them together so as to make a wood."

"Yes, you want something bolder to set off these rich, fertile foregrounds, some distant peak, some dark belt of forest, some rock cropping out here and there."

"It seems a pity to find fault when there is so much that is beautiful. Now that I can see the lake in the distance, through the trees, I could almost fancy that it is one of the lakes at home."

"You mean at Cazenovia, or Pompey?"

"No; they never came to seem like home.

I mean our old home; that was at Croydon, — Croydon, in New Hampshire. I was born there, and we lived there till my father died."

"Croydon! yes, that is a beautiful place; I was there last year."

"Oh, have you been there? Did you see it? How long did you stay?" cried Flora, now growing pale with eagerness. "Did you —" she began again, but paused, unable to say another word.

"I was on a coaching tour with a party of friends, and we drove down through Croydon on our way from Sunapee to Newport by the back road over the hills — and a rough road it was; but the views were so fine that I do not think any of us heeded that but Manning, who was worrying about his horses. However, they did it splendidly. I shall never forget that last pitch down the hill to the village of — Croydon Flats, do you call it?"

"Oh, how often I have been that way!" said the girl, with a long breath.

"Did you live up there?"

"No, we lived in the village, near the church. Perhaps you saw the house, — a white house with a garden in front, and a bow window over the porch." She looked so eager that Arthur was sorry to confess that he could not identify the house.

"There were several pretty old houses there. I did not know but that you lived in that picturesque brown house, with the hollyhocks up to the eaves, on the edge of the pond near the foot of the hill."

"Rocky-Bound, you mean; we used to go there. Father had to visit his parish all over the hills, and he used to take us too. Sometimes he took Aunt Esther, and sometimes Ida and me together; we could not all go very often, because Deacon Wilcox used to lend us his horse and chaise, and it would not hold us all. The horse had to walk all the way up that long hill, and father would take the time to teach us our lessons. He could say all the verbs from memory, and a great deal of poetry." She was talking more to herself than to her companion, and now, suddenly seeming to recollect his presence, stopped short, the fugitive color flushing her cheeks again.

"I should think the scene more congenial to poetry than verbs;" said Arthur, smiling, but it was a good-natured smile, such as is given to children from older ones who are fond of them, and seemed to put her at her ease, for she smiled back again, showing her pearls of teeth, the first time he had ever seen her smile.

"Yes, is it not lovely? And when we got to the top we always used to drive into Mrs. Welcome Partridge's; she lived in that house — did you see it? — on the right hand as you go up, just at the brow of the hill, where you can look so far off. We always used to go in there to see the view, and rest the horse, and, ask how she was, for she was a friend of Aunt Esther's. I wonder if she lives there yet. Does it look as if she did?"

"I remember the house; it is in a lovely situation, — but the only one of the family I saw was a dog who barked at us."

"Was he a large black and white dog, with long hair?"

"I think so."

"If it was Bonny, he meant no harm, — he never bites."

"No, it was a bark of friendly character, I assure you."

"But perhaps," said Flora, thoughtfully, "it was not Bonny. That was more than five years ago, and five years is a great while for a dog."

"Auntie Flora," interrupted young Orlando, "was that the dog Bonny?"

"Yes, dear, I hope so."

"Tell me how you used to make Bonny jump!"

"No, not now, Landy dear."

"But I want you to," persisted the boy.

"There is a real dog," said Flora; "look at him; and there are oxen in the barnyard."

She gave her attention to the children, who now began to be restless; for though pleased at first with the novelty of the drive, their mercurial natures would not long endure the confinement; and Arthur had to stop his horses while their places were changed, Miss Flossy clamoring for her turn at driving, much to Landy's disgust. "Girls can't drive!" he insisted, rousing his sister's wrath in return, until Flora settled the point, — whether by coaxing, or promising, or reasoning, it is difficult to say; she settled it in rather doubtful fashion, for there were renewed outbreaks of petulance from both children until the rapid motion and the warm weather lulled them to sleep, — Landy with his head on his grandmother's lap, and Flossy in her aunt's arms. Arthur would now have renewed the conversation; but Flora was silent, ashamed of having said so much in her momentary excitement. Without appearing to notice this he began to talk to her without waiting for a reply, telling her about his coaching trip and various little incidents connected with it. He had never tried so hard to please, for he would have given much to see her smile again. She did not; but there was an inspiring intentness in the way she listened, that brought back more vividly his own recollections of the lovely, lonely ways that tempt you so irresistibly to trace out their hidden windings among the heaped-up, "green-muffled" Croydon hills. He went on to describe his companions, other coaching tours, other adventures, — anything that might amuse her; yet, when his mother's house was reached again, and he watched her till she entered the door with the half-awakened children clinging to her skirts, there was something in the stately grace of her vanishing form that contrasted all the more painfully with the contracted, ill-kept surroundings, because even this poor shelter was hers only on sufferance, and he felt as if he had been almost cruel to give her an outlook into a brighter life, his life, — the one that it was in his power to take up again when he left his old home, where but few tender associations pleaded for remembrance. Yet he was beginning to perceive that the settlement of his family problems was not so simple as it had appeared to him from a distance, and that it would cost him more money than had at all entered into his calculations, and which he must give if he would not look mean in his own eyes.

Sunday morning dawned clear and bright, and Mrs. Butler had the satisfaction of putting on her carefully preserved black silk gown, and walking to church on one son's arm to hear the other preach. Neither said a word to damp her enjoyment, though Arthur would much rather have stayed at home, and Orlando, but for the impropriety of the thing, would much rather have had him. If anything was appalling to the poor fellow, it was to have Arthur for a listener, perfectly dressed, imperturbably attentive, with an air of condescending, critical civility, under which a familiar eye might perceive that he was decorously amused. Arthur, meanwhile, was mentally calculating his brother's chances of a "good parish," and concluding that they were not promising. It seemed incredible to him that Orlando could make so little of his opportunities. "He reads the Scriptures with the regular theological-seminary whine!" he thought; "and how much any one who knew how could make out of that chapter!" The prayers, too, were in the old stock phraseology; surely there were plenty of chances for telling variations at that time of day. Orlando, meanwhile, was finding some comfort in the old phrases, as so many cast-down souls have done before him, and he gave out his text and began his sermon without thinking of any one's presence, until recalled by the slight, almost imperceptible gleam of amusement in Arthur's eye, as he was reflecting that Orlando did not even put the case as well as it might be put. "How should he," he thought, — "set up in a pulpit for half an hour with no one to answer back again? I should like to hear one of these parsons pleading a case in an equity court! It would teach them something to pitch them against each other. They might at least learn to keep their audience awake!" as he regarded the comfortable slumbers of the honest farmers from the country round. Orlando's mild countenance and dejected, threadbare look gave an apologetic air to his threats of future punishment, which sounded like those he gave his own naughty children, not destined to be enforced; they lost what terrors they had with every repetition; for repeat he did till the allotted time was up, when he subsided into a short prayer, gave out a hymn, and sank down behind his pulpit with a sense of relief.

The dinner was after the usual pattern. Flora did not appear at all. She had taken pains to carry up her sister's tray before she rang the bell; for somehow, though she took herself to task for being so silly, she did not like being seen by Mr. Butler in her shabby old gown; and she could not change it till she had cleared away for the afternoon. Even then his presence seemed somehow to pervade the whole house, making her mortified as she looked around her room, with its torn paper shades and dirty towels, its broken toilet-set and table halting on three legs. How could she help it? It was called hers, but she and Orlando slept there on alternate nights, to look after Landy and Flossy, while the other slept on a sofa in Ida's room. The small box of a place was filled with the children's belongings, and her own private possessions were anywhere or nowhere. She had had no time to tidy it up that morning, as while Arthur was there a more elaborate dinner must be cooked, for which she had neither Mrs. Butler's help, nor Orlando's more efficient aid.

Aunt Esther used to say that a lady's chamber should always be in perfect order, and a stray pair of gloves or bit of string had often been made the text for a discourse in the girls' little bow windowed, wainscoted, rose-papered room at Croydon. How easy of attainment neatness had then seemed, and how Aunt Esther, when she had herself put on that paper, bought at ten cents a roll, had declared with some pride that one could have things pretty with very little money. A sense of burning shame and passionate regret brought hot tears to Flora's eyes; but she was too young yet for tears to leave their traces long, and she came downstairs "fair and fresh as rose on thorn" to find Arthur conscientiously endeavoring to make himself agreeable to his little nephew and niece, who reminded him of fireworks, so brilliantly pretty and unexpectedly explosive were they. He could think of nothing but showing them his watch, which he had tried upon Mrs. Perry's — Rosamond Curtis's — baby. They inspected it with eager and dangerous curiosity, Landy remarking that "poppa used to have one, but not such a pretty one."

"I have tried so hard not to have them catch that odious word!" thought Flora; "but they pick up everything they hear, and since Laurea came the last time they talk just as she did!" The sudden pull up of a horse and buggy at the gate, showed her that her reminiscences had been, as they often are, premonitory, and the occupants descended with great flutter of drapery and furling of sunshades.

"It's John and Almira," sighed Mrs. Butler; "I wish they wouldn't break the Sabbath so!" and her welcome to her first-born child was rather a faint one: "I am very glad to see you, John, — but couldn't you have come yesterday?"

"Not while I have my books to balance; you'll have to put up with me when you can get me, mother."

"I'm sure," said Almira, loudly, "plenty

of church members ride out on Sabbath day. We met Deacon Walsh himself, with his brother from Utica, and Mr. Murdock with a whole carriage load of his boarders."

"Dear me! dear me!" said Mrs. Butler, looking distressed.

"Well!" said John, "we've been to church this morning, anyhow."

"I always want to go to meeting twice a day, at least, only we don't have preaching in the afternoon while we've no settled minister."

"Land got the job this morning, didn't he?" said John, looking at his brother, who was endeavoring to restrain his children's vehement attentions to their gorgeously arrayed cousin.

"Perhaps the children had better go out to play," he suggested, mildly.

"Well!" said Mrs. John Butler, doubtfully, "only the last time they took Laurea out to play, they put sand and ashes in her hair, and it took me no end of time to get it out. But one can't hear themselves talk with them in the room. Get an apron for her, Florer, will you? And if she could have one of their old hats —"

Flora produced a decayed straw hat of her

own, and Mrs. John removed her daughter's bangles, ear-rings, and locket, remarking that them young ones would smash everything up.

"I don't think they ought to play out doors, Sabbath afternoon," said the grandmother, troubled. "Can't they sit down quietly, like good little children?"

Whether the youthful Orlando and Flora could perform the feat alluded to, may be doubted; the fact remained that they never had; and no one seeming inclined to take their instruction in hand, they were allowed to depart, dragging with them the transformed Laurea, half reluctant, half eager for the mad course of adventures into which her cousins were wont to lead her on her "Sabbath" visits; and Flora placed herself near the window, where she was supposed to accomplish the feat, trying to the powers of a conjurer, of "keeping her eye upon them."

"I suppose you went to meetin'," resumed John, addressing himself to Arthur.

"I did."

"And how were you pleased with the exercises?"

"Very well," replied Arthur, in a tone which precluded further questioning.

"I tell Orlando," said John's wife, "he ought to speak up more; folks like to hear a man preach as if he were after somethin', — not but what I like all he says well enough. And how's Ider? I most forgot to ask."

"A little better, we hope," replied Orlando.

"Can I go up and see her?"

"I am afraid she is hardly able to-day," said Flora; "you see it is the afternoon, and she gets tired by afternoon."

"Yes, and when I come in the morning she is never ready to see any one. She'll never be any better while you keep her so shut up; she ought to see folks and be cheered up a little. And how's the baby? I can see him, I s'pose."

"He is asleep now."

"Well he'd better be let alone then, I should say. The last time I was here that young one commenced to yell as soon as it woke, and kept it up two mortal hours — as long as I stayed. If I had him I'd soon stop him; but you coddle him and spoil him."

"Did you enjoy the sermon this morning?" asked her mother-in-law.

"Not much! Dr. Todd is gettin' old and played-out, I guess. We haven't anythin' goin' on now. If I was the deacons, I'd make him get up somethin'; we'd ought to be havin' a revival before this time, if he means to stay."

"Come now, Almirer!" said her husband, "Dr. Todd is a pretty good sort of a man; I like his sermons."

"Well, you needn't talk — they haven't converted you yet," said Almira, with a laugh.

"Yes," said Mrs. Butler; "I wish I could see the boys anxious! Perhaps," in a low tone to her daughter-in-law; "you could persuade John to have a little talk with Orlando. Orlando, couldn't you say a few words to John while he's here? You might step out with him. I hope you have improved your chances to drop a word in season to Arthur, besides what he heard from the pulpit."

All three of the brothers looked for a moment extremely uncomfortable, but in a moment more Arthur could not restrain a smile, and even the unfortunate Orlando looked feebly amused, while John burst into a hearty laugh. "No, mother, thank you; 'tain't fair to set Land on to any of the family out of hours. What's that? A new picture, I declare; look there, Almirer."

"Yes," said Mrs. Butler; "it's a present from a rich Episcopalian lady Arthur knows in Boston."

"Art is makin' up to a rich old maid," said Jonah, who had escaped his mother's admonitions, owing to his elders being present.

"Indeed!" said Mrs. John; "I admire his taste. Why, Florer, they'll be a match for you and your old beau. How's his courtship gettin' along?"

"You should not say such things, Almira," said Mrs. Butler, looking the perplexed distress she often felt in the company of her daughter-in-law, whose vulgarity repelled her own refined instincts, though in her simplicity she thought it the usual manifestation of the worldliness and fashion which, she sometimes feared, showed Almira, though a professing Christian, to be in danger of cherishing a false hope. "Dr. Griscom admires Flora, and thinks her a very superior young lady, but it is so long now that I don't think he has any idea of marrying again."

"Trust an old widower lookin' out for number three, for knowin' better than that!" said Almira; "but I'm afraid he's after money, hey, Florer? You better not let him get wind of your old lady, Arthur, though very likely if she can get you, she won't take him."

"The picture seems to be a sacred subject," said Mrs. Butler, eager to stop this talk; "I thought the lady might have painted it, but Arthur says it's a chromo."

"It's Japanese, ain't it?" said Mrs. John.

"I don't think so," said Mrs. Butler; "there are Latin words on the back."

"Well, it looks Japanese. It's a queer thing, anyhow."

"Read it, Flora," said Mrs. Butler; "you can read Latin."

"Angels of the blessed Angelico of Fiesole," read Flora, carelessly; "it is not Latin, Mrs. Butler, but Italian, I think."

"Lord! how many lingoes can you read?" asked Mrs. John.

"I never learned Italian; but it is very like Latin."

"Flora reads Latin and Greek too, very well," said Mrs. Butler; "her father taught her. She reads the Greek Testament sometimes, at family prayers, and it sounds most interesting."

"Please, Mrs. Butler —" said Flora,

imploringly, and for the first time showing some dislike to being made the theme of discussion. Somewhat to Arthur's surprise, she had not appeared to mind Mrs. John Butler's railleries at all, but had preserved a silence too indifferent to be disdainful. Flora disliked being in the same room with Almira so much that nothing the latter said or did could increase or diminish the sensation; but this was a very different matter.

"Never mind, Florer," said John, good-humoredly, "you're pretty enough not to be hurt by it, anyhow. Come, Art, don't you want to stretch your legs a bit?"

"We'd ought to be goin' home," said Almira; "I'll hunt up Laurea."

"Won't you stay to tea?" said Mrs. Butler, in a quavering voice, apparently divided between fears of an acceptance or refusal.

"That's what we come for," said John.

"Really, John —" expostulated his wife.

"Why, I don't git out to mother's any too often; you wouldn't have us go back with nothin' but a call, would you? We'll be back in a minute;" and he walked off, followed by Arthur, while Orlando, who had not been asked, and who knew that they had gone off to discuss him and his affairs, remained at home to help Flora blow up the fire and get tea, — a process materially hindered by what Mrs. John had termed the baby's "yells" from above, — not to speak of sounds from the other children that more justly deserved the name. Almira preserved the supreme indifference of "company" as she sat with Mrs. Butler in the parlor, the elder lady in vain endeavoring, with occasional remarks of a religious tendency, to stem the tide of the younger's catalogue of her new clothes, broken only by the recurring observation that "if them young ones was hers, she would train them well."

CHAPTER VI.

JOHN and Arthur, meanwhile, were going over the same circuitous course they had traversed on Friday morning; the only new feature was a promise from John that he would see Jonah safe out of Syracuse, on any road but that leading to Liverpool, with ten dollars in his pocket, supplied by Arthur, to seek for agricultural employment; for, as John remarked, the farmers would take anybody at that time of year, though "their keepin' him was another matter." They did not get so far in relation to Orlando, as one brother was determined not to ask any aid, and the other not to offer any.

It was not until they had nearly reached home that John, with a sidelong, curious look, asked abruptly, "Do you think Florer Shepherd a pretty girl?"

"I should hardly call her so."

"Possible? Well, Almirer won't allow she is; but then, you know women don't set any by each other's good looks. I don't s'pose you'd call Ider pretty, either, then?"

"Do you think her so?"

"Why, yes! a good many folks think her prettier than Florer; but somehow there's somethin' about Florer — I don't know what it is —"

"Not prettiness, certainly," said Arthur, who had no wish to go on at cross purposes, "Miss Shepherd is the most beautiful girl I have ever seen."

"Indeed!" said John, with a meaning intonation; but as he received no encouragement to proceed, he went on to think to himself that if Arthur should be taken with Flora, it would be an excellent thing for Orlando and his family, and indirectly for himself as well, since the chief part of their support must then undoubtedly fall upon Arthur; and that so desirable a consummation might be made more sure, he resolved not to hint at it to his wife, whose dislike to the young lady might lead her to interfere with it, — not that he blamed Almira so much; for there was no denying that "she's full of her airs," he finished, half unconsciously, aloud. Arthur looked still more indifferent, and John reflected that probably the airs would not be put on to his brother. They reached home in time for a family tea, at which Almira questioned Arthur, in a jocose way, about Miss Curtis, whose name she had obtained from Mrs. Butler, and Mrs. Butler, whose ideas grew more secular at sundown, occasionally put in a word. Mrs. John said it was funny for an old maid to have so much money, and wondered how she could use it. Mrs. Butler hoped she gave a great deal away to good objects, — she supposed the Episcopalians had missionaries of their own.

"Lives in a house, and keeps a girl, does she? Don't she have anybody else livin' with her?" asked Almira.

"Not all the time. She often has friends."

"I should think she'd feel lonely when her help leave her," said Mrs. Butler, who regarded "help" as nomads by race.

"I never knew her to be without servants."

"Does she keep more than one?" asked Mrs. John.

"Yes."

"How many?"

"I don't know," said Arthur, like the most unwilling witness he had ever cross-questioned. "I only know two or three of them by sight; but of course there are others."

"Goodness gracious! how big is her house?"

"Her town house is not very large."

"Town house! how many has she?"

"Only three that she lives in."

Mrs. John was fairly silenced for a moment, and Arthur, as he remembered that he had been dining with Miss Curtis on Wednesday, could hardly believe that it was so little while ago. He always felt, when in company with John and his wife, that there must be a weak spot in his own social armor, carefully as it had been braced and girded. How could he look around the table and picture himself bringing Sophy there in the character of one of the family? Only Flora offered a suggestion of any possible point of contact. The Curtises, surely, could see nothing amiss in Mrs. Orlando Butler's sister; and it was to be hoped that Mrs. Orlando might not be unlike her.

That evening, when the John Butlers had driven off, and Arthur, on the back porch, was watching through the budding elm-branches the young moon rising in a clear cool sky, the one vision of beauty which had satisfied his boyish cravings, disgusted with the cramped surroundings below, a low voice at his elbow said, "Mr. Butler."

"Miss Shepherd! I beg your pardon!" and he sprang up from the bench on which he had been sitting, and offered her his place, which she took without hesitation, and he sat down beside her, wondering what she could want with him, and his heart beating with expectation of — he did not know what.

"Mr. Butler, I only wanted to say that Ida and I have a few things — I mean books and furniture — that might be worth something if they could be sold. When we left Croydon we sold some of our things there, but some Aunt Esther wanted to keep, and Deacon Wilcox stored them in his barn; and they are there now. We meant to send for them after Ida was married and we took the house at Cazenovia, but it was not seen to, and we moved again so soon; the silver we brought with us, and it is here now; there is not much of it, but it might bring something —"

"My dear Miss Shepherd! you must not think of such a thing!"

"But I really think we ought. You see it has cost so much to have so much sickness. Orlando would never speak of it himself, but I think it would be a relief to his mind. Father had some nice books, and Aunt Esther always said the furniture was good. It is very pretty old mahogany. I don't suppose it would sell for much in Croydon, but would it not be a good plan to have it sent down to Boston? — if you could only see about it."

"It depends on the condition of the market, and the time of year, and so many other things," said Arthur, slowly deliberating. "I would not do anything about it just now, at any rate;" and seeing that she looked unsatisfied, he went on: "I will certainly see about it when I think it is best; but you must not let any one else have anything to do with it."

"I will not, then," said Flora, reluctantly.

"You could not find any one who would attend to it as well as I could; promise me that you will be sure to consult me first about it in any case."

Flora looked a little surprised, but gave the promise without further discussion, and Arthur felt relieved at the thought that he had prevented the girl from stripping herself of her few possessions; but suddenly struck with an idea, he exclaimed, "But your sister — I suppose she has an equal share in them?"

"Ida would do anything that you thought — that I thought was right."

He was afraid she would go away now, but she sat silently on, the first time he had seen her sit still; indeed she rarely had the chance. There was as much grace in her motionless rest as there was repose in her quickest movement. He racked his brains for something to say that might keep her, but to his surprise they gave no response. The fact was that unless he could do something for her, idle admiration and gallantry seemed useless; and what can a man of thirty-two do for a girl of nineteen, unless he can do the one thing that is everything? He had had some idea of beseeching Miss Curtis's good offices for her. Perhaps that lady, who liked to give in a private and personal way, and who was always pleased with good looks in her *protegées*, would ask Flora to come and fit herself for something or other in Boston, under her own eye, as she had asked plenty of other girls less attractive; and Sophy, he thought with pride, was much too high-minded to feel any idle jealousy of another girl's beauty. But as he looked at Flora now, transfigured by the April moonlight, the plan seemed less feasible. He doubted whether there were not too much of the desirable quality in question here, and he feared that it would be awkward; that Miss Curtis would hardly believe — that he could hardly explain just the degree and kind of interest he felt. No matter what he said beforehand, she would still be surprised when she saw Flora. He shrank from putting his vague thoughts in words, even to himself; but he was just telling himself again that there was nothing but pity and admiration in them, if he could only make other people understand him, when the baby's faint cry came from above, and Flora was on her feet, and half-way up the stairs before the second sound.

Arthur sauntered back to his lodgings, provoked that he had not had himself driven into Syracuse that evening to take the early Monday train for Boston. There was plenty of work that he could have done Monday evening, and he gained nothing by staying but another desultory morning at his mother's house, pervaded by a discomfort yet more pronounced than usual, as befitted washing-day; and where he had the doubtful pleasure of watching Flora doing the family washing in the back yard. No exercise could display to more advantage the nymph-like grace of her form; but the satisfaction it gave his eye was perhaps more than counterbalanced by his irritation at seeing her scrubbing away on Jonah's greasy shirts and muddy stockings.

> "Her yellow hair was braided in a tress,
>   Behind her back a yarde long, I guess;"

and as he gazed from the window, unseen himself, half feeling that he ought not, and yet unable to leave off, Master Orlando, passing behind her, caught the loose curling end thereof, and gave it a sudden hard pull that made her throw back her head with a start and frown of pain, and raise one dripping hand to relieve the shock by grasping the thick heavy plait at the roots.

"This is too much!" soliloquized Arthur, who in a moment more stood beside her, and seized the little culprit by the arm. "You are a very naughty boy," he said severely; "and if your father does not punish you as he ought for being so rude to your aunt, I will."

"Landy did not mean to be naughty, did he?" said Flora; "he did not know that it would hurt Auntie." She bent down and held out her arms to the boy, who ran into them, looking round at his uncle with the defiant scowl of the incipient man who sees some one coming between him and his own particular piece of feminine property; but as Flora murmured some sweet indistinct expostulations in his ear, the scowl relaxed into as thorough a smile, and he pursed up his rosy mouth to meet hers, pressing her cheeks between the chubby palms of his dimpled hands, making so lovely a group, that Arthur's "You will spoil those children, Miss Shepherd," came softened into half rallying admiration. But Flora took it seriously.

"I hope not," she said. "Landy tries to be good. Don't you, Landy?"

"I *are* good," said Landy, now passing his hand tenderly over the rich rippling locks, whose own thickness made them stand up like an aureole where they rolled back from her face, — but with a sparkle of mischief deep in his eyes as he looked toward Arthur, which suggested, "If you say a word, I'll do it again."

"You may come with me, if you are good," said Arthur, impressively; and as Master Landy, though somewhat inclined to accept any offer put in the form of a reward, seemed doubtful as to how much real enjoyment it might promise, he rashly added the bribe of his pocket note-book with pencil attached, and having torn out the written pages, abandoned the whole to the little boy and his sister, who hovered fairy-like in the background. Flora was at liberty to go on with her work; and as she bent over the washtub again, big tears splashed into the water. What could make her so silly? She was always crying since Mr. Butler came. For one reason, things had gone so awry, as they always do whenever you are anxious about them. She had never known the children behave so badly; generally they minded her very — no, perhaps it was more truthful to say, pretty well. She swallowed her tears in a hurry and raised a fairly cheerful countenance to meet Orlando, who came out of the kitchen to bring her a pail of hot water.

"Why, Flora, are you tired, poor child? It is too bad we have such a big wash this week; I'll wring out the clothes, for it's time to get dinner, and I suppose we must have dinner if Arthur's going to stay for it," went on Orlando, who, arrayed in his morning costume with apron, a shade worse than usual for Mondays, proceeded without a thought of incongruity to put the tattered clothes through the rickety old wringer. "I wish," he thought, but did not say, "that Arthur had left last night. If he minds Flora's working so hard, I wonder he did not think of to-day being washing-day. Why did he stay, I wonder?"

"Why, indeed?" thought Arthur, as he finally found himself comfortably settled in a sleeping-car section on the Grand Central Railroad eastward bound. Why indeed had he come at all? He had not accomplished anything by it, — nay, had involved himself in more expense, which he could ill afford. The invisible Ida, strong in her weakness, had proved too powerful an adversary. What gentleman can turn his invalid sister-in-law out of her bed and out of doors, no matter how much she may abuse the privileges of her position? And he felt the hot blood rush to his face as he recalled certain appealing looks and tones by which Flora had shown that she felt afraid of him and entreated his forbearance. He had always felt more self-satisfaction in his politeness to women, carried to the very extreme of old-fashioned courtesy than in anything else in his demeanor; and here was the most beautiful one he had ever seen, regarding him as if she were an aged pauper, and he a landlord ready to evict her and hers at the slightest notice. Never had a visit to his family, always an uncomfortable piece of duty, been so unbearable; and he resolved that for the future he would communicate with them by letter. It should be two years, at least, before he set foot in Liverpool again.

He felt surprised when he reached Boston on Tuesday morning to find how short a time after all, he had been away; but he found enough to do in catching up with the accumulated work of the last four days. He had not a moment to think, with the press of business, — prospects of more, promises of success that might make him able to stand his increased expenses for his family, and yet realize his own hopes without what would now be a most mortifying delay. It was only working a little harder; and he bent every nerve, already strained to its apparent utmost, yet throbbing with a sense of reserved strength, like a race-horse within sight of the goal. Time flew; his conditional engagement to dine with Miss Curtis and escort her and Sophy to the Apollo Club concert must go. Never mind, — he could meet them there and explain; and in the interval at the middle of the concert he was slowly walking down the middle aisle of the crowded Music Hall, cool, well-dressed, and deliberate as ever. He knew Miss Curtis would be sure to have managed to get into seats at the end of the row, so that he could pause and talk to them.

Why did the well-known scene, the familiar faces, look strange and dim? He was tired with his journey perhaps; at any rate he was stupidly passing the very pair he was in search of, when Miss Curtis's voice, close at his elbow, recalled him to himself, and he turned sharply round, confused at his unwonted awkwardness. Yes, there she was, smiling a good-natured welcome as she held out her hand, and there was Sophy by her side, more shyly extending hers. He shook hands with both, struggling with a longing to rush out of the hall — out of the town — out of the world if he could; for he knew now, and knew it with a pang of shame and sorrow, that he could never love — could never marry — Sophy Curtis.

He managed, he hardly knew how, to get through the polite greeting proper to the occasion. He thought he did it very well, but something must have struck them in his manner; for Miss Curtis's own grew more formal by a shade, faint, but perceptible, and Sophy's answers were low and short as she turned and returned the leaves of her programme. Thank Heaven! the interval was over at last, the performers collecting on the stage again, and he could with propriety excuse himself, and hurry somewhere — anywhere out of sight — to the darkest corner of the hall under the balcony, and while standing motionless and silent as if wholly absorbed in the music, try to realize how utterly his life was changed, and that from this moment he must walk a different way, and follow another light. He knew that he could never, as long as he lived, forget that first dawning look of doubt and wonder in Sophy's eyes; and he knew too that by and-by it would rouse an unending remorse, — but not now, while a tenor voice was singing Reichardt's "Image of the Rose," and his whole being was yearning for a look into a pair of blue eyes, and the clasp of a little hand that had hardly touched him in passing. Fool that he had been! he had driven twenty miles by Flora's side, and sat by her under warranting moonlight, and feasted his eyes on her beauty, without knowing that he could not live without her.

The concert was over, and the audience rose. It was Arthur's privilege always to see Miss Curtis to her carriage, — half the time to be taken as far as his own lodgings. He could not stir; he saw the ladies, after waiting a moment, rise, and Miss Curtis look round; saw one of a hundred young fellows of her acquaintance, it did not matter who, step forward in his stead; saw her incline to hold back — to wait — and Sophy, eagerly determined, and well he could guess why, to hurry the party on and out of the hall. Poor Sophy! her dreams that night could not be pleasant ones.

CHAPTER VII.

AS for Arthur, he only got himself to sleep sometime in the morning by resolving that he would take the Wednesday night train for Liverpool again; but he did not, and the middle of June found him still in Boston. Things looked very different when he woke to the work-a-day world from which he had wandered by moonlight with music ringing in his ears. His love was as strong as ever. There was no question of any struggle between it and worldly considerations. He took no merit to himself for the unselfishness of his devotion, because he knew he could not help himself; nay, he felt a good many honest regrets, vain though he knew they were, for the good things he was leaving on one side; and sharper pangs for Sophy's sake, not unmixed with mortification that he had so suddenly been taken captive by mere outward loveliness. Of course, Flora was a good girl, or there was no truth in faces; but neither she nor any one else could be better than Sophy.

He delayed the inevitable action that he knew must come, because he must have all his plans and prospects as carefully mapped out before he struggled to utter his passion at Flora's feet as when he had meditated that well-expressed, dignified, well-assured proposal to Sophy. His ability to marry was much the same in both cases. Sophy would have had no great sum to start with; but her father would have given her a house and an outfit, and her mother, who had a nice little fortune of her own, would have supplied all gaps left in the abundant gifts of her relations and friends. He knew in what style such things had been done for Rosamond Curtis, and Sophy could have had no less. Flora would have none of this; but then, she would expect nothing, whereas it would have cost a pretty penny to keep Sophy as she, or rather her family, would expect her to be kept.

The disposal of his own family weighed more on his mind, though it was really easier in this case than in the other. His mother, he now resolved, must live with him, — a thing he had always regarded as impossible, and he knew that at the best there must be many rubs between them; but Mrs. Butler was fond of Flora, and Flora seemed fond of her, — that would be a link. He would pay up Orlando's debts, and give him the use of the house in Liverpool for a fixed term, until he could find a parish. He had an opportunity of doing the thing more cheaply on the face of it, by getting a clerk's place for his brother in Boston, where his recommendation would secure to good character and willingness to work a salary, small, but larger than the preacher's stipend had yet been; but he dismissed the idea, thinking that it would never do to have Orlando's family so near himself and his wife: there would be no end to what they would get out of him through her.

Probably he could not have waited so long if he had not felt so secure of Flora. He did not dream of being loved by her; she seemed to him too young and unawakened to have thought of such a thing; but how delicious it would be to woo her love with delights of soft services and caressing courtesy! Hers should be another sort of life when she was his! He had no apprehension as to any other possible lover. He did not believe there was a young man in Liverpool whom she would look at, even if she had the time. Dr. Griscom, indeed, might be a rival more to be feared. Flora might be willing — he could not blame her if she were — to marry the first not utterly uncongenial wooer who came, to escape her present life of drudgery; and though the doctor was sixty-odd and had never been handsome, yet elderly widowers, he well knew, have an advantage in experience which frequently carries the day with youth and beauty. But though Arthur did not know Flora well enough to be sure of her here, he did know the doctor, who indeed had brought him into the world, and whom he judged to be about the last man of his acquaintance to make the blunder that such a match would be. He toiled on, doing the work of ten, till late in June, when he felt he could leave town with some prospect of being able to stay away a week at least; he ought to make all arrangements, for of course he did not want to go back again but once; and he had his eye on a pretty cottage in Newton Centre, where he could take his bride directly, content to economize a few years out of society, in which he felt, did he make the attempt to keep up with it, he must occupy a very different place from what he had done, and still more from what he had hoped to do; and he felt some satisfaction, not in making a sacrifice for Flora's sake, but in paying the penalty for his inconstancy to Sophy. Gladly would he have made any confession or atonement; but how confess where confession were an insult, and how atone where atonement were a mockery? He took what he thought the best course by silently withdrawing himself from all intercourse with her, with all due attention to ceremony. He declined the Curtises' invitations, always giving good and sufficient reason, and called when he knew they were all out. He soon perceived that the other side had taken the alarm, by the gradual slackening of the attentions once so freely lavished; and when Miss Curtis left town, unseen by him for a fortnight at least, he received a rather formal invitation from her to spend a week at her sea-side house at Gloucester, — the time specified, to him, who had once known that he could come and go there at his pleasure! It was with one of the sharpest pangs he ever endured that he wrote a refusal in terms carefully chosen to correspond. He knew that he was rejecting one of the most precious things of his life; and the worst part of it was the knowledge that the suffering must come hardest on those to whom he owed it. He did not know which had the most right to think him ungrateful; though Miss Curtis was more of a personal loss to him, and he believed he should be to her.

She was, indeed, quite as wretched about the matter as he could imagine, being in the miserable position into which a warm-hearted person accustomed to interfere beneficently in her neighbor's affairs is thrown when action in any direction is impossible without doing harm. If things had only not been at just the pass they were! If Arthur's courtship of Sophy had been more incipient, so that she could with affected ignorance boldly ask the reason for his change of manner on the score of her own old friendship; or more declared, so that she could have questioned either of them, in the chance of a misunderstanding, — there would have been something to be done, at least; but now, for Sophy's sake, there was nothing for it but to hold her tongue, and see the girl looking pale and anxious without remark; while a mutual consciousness made them drop by degrees all mention of his name. She made what feeble effort was in her power by inviting Arthur as much as she decently could, only to be repelled by his exquisitely courteous notes of regrets and excuses in which no flaw could be discerned. She inquired a little of others, but very discreetly, and with no satisfactory result. Arthur Butler, she heard, was working hard, and looked worn and harassed. There might be some family or business complication; she longed to ask, but she had not been wont to sue for his confidence; she had no chance of seeing him alone, and she could not bring herself to write, — time, meanwhile, slipping away like running water. Before the first of June she had left town for her country seat in Vermont, where she had enlarged and beautified her great-grandfather's old farmhouse, and where a lively party of cousins now assembled; but not Sophy, who said that she must go and help Rosamond settle in the cottage which the Perrys had taken at Cohasset. They were gone, and Arthur breathed more freely till the day when he could get away from Boston himself.

Midsummer night was warm, very warm at Liverpool, where Arthur was not in the least expected, for he thought it best to give no warning. The house was still, and there was an unwonted feeling of space about it, for Jonah was still away, and Orlando had gone to Geneseo. The dead quiet of the evening gave the feeling of a coming storm, and Flora, as she went on her late way upstairs, wondered, with some dim idea of correspondence in the moral world, whether something were not about to happen. But she had had this sensation, natural to youth, a great many times, and nothing ever had happened. She supposed Mr. Butler's visit had unsettled her, and it was not likely that he would come again. She set her lamp on a table in the narrow passage at the head of the stairs, careful that no ray might hit the eyes of any of the sleepers within the half-open doors, and entering her sister's darkened room, sat down on the foot of her narrow couch by the baby's crib, and gave a loose rein to the doubtful luxury of thought, on topics which were hardly of an enlivening nature. Things were going on in the usual weary way, Ida not much better and the baby not much worse. It might improve when cool weather came again, but the summer that must first be lived through would make a good half of its small existence. Orlando's prospects of employment were still doubtful, and the expenses would mount up to a frightful sum in spite of all she could do to keep them down. On observing that no item of the weekly account indicated that a servant had been engaged, Arthur had written peremptory orders that one was to be immediately hired; but Flora had as peremptorily refused to have anything to do with one, and as she was on the spot she carried her point with Orlando, who did not know how to take the initiative in the matter without her help. Mr. Butler, she thought, had no business to concern himself so much about her. She was strong and healthy, and had never complained to him nor to any one else. If he had spoken to her about it her answer would have been ready. She wanted to make him feel as he ought, and to show it — just once.

That just once might be sufficient was probable, for as she bent over the baby she murmured in the softest tone the word "Arthur!" There was no harm in using the little fellow's name, but she started guiltily and looked with alarm through the dimness to see if Ida were awake. But her sister slept serenely, and Flora, kneeling by the little crib, buried her flushed face in the cool, white pillows. Baby was her confidant, the only one she had, and a safe and sufficient one. She rarely went so far as to say anything to him, but she could think and dream when she had him in her arms, or lay down by him as she did now, with her hand ready to soothe him off when he stirred. As might be supposed, dreams soon won the victory over thoughts.

Arthur, meanwhile, was repeating his journey of two months ago, wondering that he had gone through it then so carelessly. He did not go near his brother John's, but set out as soon as he left the train at Syracuse, to walk the five miles in the fresh dewy morning. It had rained in the night, as it had promised, and soft wreathing mists and dew, reflecting sunrise skies, made everything lovely, even where the way, under the glare of noon, might have looked hard and bare enough. The glamour, he knew, was partly in his own eyes, and at times, through all his eagerness, faint misgivings attacked him lest it might prove as fleeting as the day-dawn. Should he find Flora as beautiful as memory painted her? Had any awkwardness, any vulgarity about her passed unnoticed in the blaze of light? The signs of intellect or heart that had glowed through the calm radiance of her presence — might they not be partly in his own ardent desire? How much of a divinity should he find his marble goddess, once melted into flesh and blood? He had plenty of time for these fears and jealousies of love while engaging his former lodgings, dressing, and then strolling about aimlessly till he knew they would be through breakfast at his mother's; but when he could fairly allow that it was late enough, and walk, this time with a beating heart, up the little path between beds where feeble attempts at gardening had resulted in an abundant crop of weeds, which overhung the little-used way to the front door, marking with muddy smears his immaculate boots and trousers, and Flora herself had opened the door, he felt ashamed of his faithlessness to the very depths of his soul. How much lovelier she was than he had dared to picture her! But surely, in these two months, she had grown more lovely. With how refined a grace she met him, blushing a little, but no more than the suddenness of his appearance might well excuse.

"How do you do, Miss Shepherd? I hope you are all well?"

"Thank you, we hope Ida is a little better; but the baby is still very poorly."

"I am sorry," said Arthur, who was thinking how maddeningly sweet was her low voice, especially with the mournful fall at the close; then, as he followed her into the parlor, which had its usual shut-up air: "You must not let me be in your way."

"Oh, no; Mrs. Butler will be very glad to see you. Orlando has gone to Geneseo, but we expect him back to-morrow." She was hurrying away, when Arthur said, catching at something to detain her: "I hope you have everything you want, and all the advice you need for the baby?"

"Yes, indeed," said Flora, "Dr. Griscom is very kind. He comes almost every day." Arthur, looking at her, felt that perhaps he had credited the doctor with too much good sense; but what did it matter? He was here now, ready to bear down a stronger rival, if need be, and another look at her unconscious face made him ashamed again. "I will tell Mrs. Butler you are here," she went on, as she left the room, and Mrs. Butler, after a hasty toilet, came in, nervous and apprehensive at her son's sudden appearance, and exhausted herself with apologies, mingled with hints, as skilfully put as she knew how, to find out why he came.

"I wish," she said, "you 'd stop — I mean come back — to dinner, Arthur; though, to be sure, we have n't much of a dinner to ask you to; we did n't think of having meat, as we did n't expect any of the men-folks to be here. Orlando is at Geneseo; he has gone to apply for a place in the excellent academy there, and we greatly hope he will succeed; and Jonah — you know that Jonah is working on a farm near Fabius?"

"Yes; I hope he will stick to it."

"Mr. Hewson is a wealthy farmer, I believe, he does not give Jonah much wages, but Jonah seems to like it there pretty well. I believe the family are very kind to him."

Arthur, inattentive to anything except that there was no immediate prospect of

Master Jonah's return, bade his mother good-by, and departed, promising to come back to dinner, and seeing that she would rather be relieved of his presence in the interim. He knew that it was vain to expect to get a word with Flora in the morning, but perhaps in the afternoon it might be managed. He could neither eat nor sleep till he had had it over, and he felt that it was going to be a terribly hard matter to get it over. But once let him make the beginning which her unconsciousness rendered so difficult, and he was sure of success, — prepared for, and indeed ready to enjoy any amount of shyness and coyness. She should not be frightened, or hurried; he could control himself, and taste the full sweetness of pleasures not too rashly spent.

CHAPTER VIII.

ARTHUR came back punctually at the dinner hour, and entering this time by the back door, made his way past the empty kitchen to the little dining-room. There, upon the shabby old lounge where Jonah used to loll at full length, now reclined on piles of pillows the very different person of Mrs. Orlando Butler, who looked up as he came in, and extended a slender little hand in friendly greeting before her sister had time to introduce him. "I am so glad!" she said, "to meet you at last, and to thank you so much for all your great kindness."

"Don't speak of it," said Arthur, surprised at this beginning; "it is I who am fortunate to have an opportunity of meeting you at last;" and he looked with some intentness at Flora's sister, whom "some folks" thought the "prettier" of the two. As beautiful, he at once saw she never could have been, even before illness had robbed her of her bloom. She could never have had the same regal mould of face and figure, though she might have had the same brilliant coloring, and still possessed as lovely a pair of blue eyes. Perhaps the charm lay in the greater degree of consciousness, without a particle of vanity or forwardness, which made her loveliness appeal more powerfully to the beholder. Landy and Flossy hung over the back of their mother's sofa, and Flora sat on a low stool by her side. The baby was quiet upstairs, having slept more of late, and the group was a fair one to contemplate.

"Say 'How do you do?' to your uncle, children," said the mother.

"Do you remember me?" asked Arthur, condescendingly.

"Oh, yes!" cried Landy; "you took us to ride! Will you take us to ride again?"

"Landy!" said Ida, reprovingly; then turning to Arthur, "Poor little things, they so seldom get a ride. They have talked of that one ever since."

"I hope I can, while I am here," said Arthur, conscious that all this was part of his *rôle;* "and I have brought you something too; can you guess what it is?"

"A horse!" shouted Landy, and then stopped, struck dumb at his own prescience, as a magnificent steed with flowing mane and tail made its appearance from a large parcel; while Flossy raised her head from the sofa pillow, where it had presented nothing but a mass of fluffy yellow curls, and accepted a French doll which looked as if it were modelled after her own self. Both children, in their ecstasy, gave vehement thanks without being reminded to do so, to their aunt's secret satisfaction.

The dinner was the liveliest meal Arthur remembered in his mother's house, owing to the little streak of mercury in Ida's composition. She suddenly collapsed into weariness afterward, and must be taken upstairs, helped, indeed actually carried, by Arthur, while Flora followed with her cushions, and together they settled her comfortably. One beauty thanked him with a smile, and the other with a sigh; and as he went downstairs he allowed it to be very natural that Flora should want to help her sister; he would not stint her in making presents, so long as the Orlando Butlers kept themselves and their poverty at a distance. It was a pity, but how could it be helped? Orlando had no business to marry that pretty creature if he could not support her better.

"I think Mr. Butler is so very nice!" Ida was saying to Flora upstairs, in a tone of some surprise; "he is not a bit like John."

"Who ever said he was?"

"I don't know, — what made me think so was that you never said anything about him at all." She paused a moment, and then went on decisively: "He is a great deal more like Orlando than he is like John — don't you think so?" she asked, confident, as invalids are apt to be, of receiving an answer where speaking is such an effort.

"No; I don't think he is like either of them."

"Well!" said Ida, wearily, "he carried me upstairs very like Orlando, at any rate, — *almost* as nicely!"

All this, Arthur thought, might be a very pretty way of conducting a courtship for one less in a hurry than he was. But his mind was set on business, and he managed to say to Flora, when she came downstairs again, "Can you spare me a few moments, Miss Shepherd, this afternoon? There is something I want very much to say to you."

"Oh, yes! I shall be very glad!" she

replied, with an eagerness in her manner that rather surprised him.

"To you alone,—please say nothing to any one else about it."

"Of course not," she answered promptly, and Arthur, rather taken aback at her readiness, thought he might as well be explicit on every point and went on: "I don't want the children about."

"No," said Flora, decidedly: "they would understand everything, and go right and tell Ida before we were ready. I have errands in the village this afternoon; will you come with me?"

"With the greatest pleasure," replied Arthur, though he could have wished to tell his love out of sight and hearing of the gossip of Liverpool; and determining to give the meeting a chance air, he proceeded: "Let me know at what time you will be through with your errands, and I will meet you."

"As near four as I can," said Flora, carelessly; and then as she was leaving the room, she turned, with her hand on the door, to say with her usual grave earnestness of manner: "Did you really come on for—I mean partly for this? You are very kind."

She vanished, leaving him perplexed as to whether it were childish simplicity that could not, or coquetry that would not, understand what he meant. What could she be thinking of, or what could she imagine he was thinking of? Four o'clock found him on a bench on the green, commanding a convenient view of the village emporium, and at half-past, or nearly so, she appeared on her way there, like a sculptured goddess, all ivory and gold. She wore her best gown, of a cheap soft cream-white material known to commerce as cheese-cloth, made by herself as plainly as possible, and with no particular fit. The fit, like that of the draperies of a Greek statue, was in the putting on. On her head was set a large hat of the kind called palmleaf, and worn by farm-laborers at work, which she had twisted into shapeliness, and wreathed with a piece like her gown. A great bunch of field daisies was stuck in her belt, and she carried a willow market-basket. Arthur, though discerning and fastidious as to woman's attire, thought hers a marvel of effectiveness, and wondered where she could have got it. She went into the shop scarcely glancing his way, and as she came out again, after what appeared to him an interminable time, he advanced, and took her basket, now no light weight; but instead of retaining it, he handed it to a little barefoot boy, whom he astonished by the gift of a quarter of a dollar, and orders to take the basket to Mrs. Butler's. Flora looked on with some surprise, but said nothing, and when at the first turn they came to Arthur said, "Let us go home this way, it is longer," she followed him down a side street, which soon became a road, and appeared to branch independently off into the country, though both knew that a circuit could be made which would bring them home again. Not a soul was in sight about the few straggling houses on the way, whose front rooms were hermetically sealed and shaded; not a lounger was out at so early an hour. No one met them but Dr. Griscom coming back from a call fifteen miles away, doubled up half asleep in his easy buggy, while his bay mare, the best in Onondaga County, picked her own way at an even trot, and looked intelligently at the young couple, to whom her master, suddenly raising his hat, bowed with a knowing smile.

Flora never seemed to notice it, but

walked on like an obedient child. Somehow this submission took the zest from love-making, and made it more difficult of beginning; but Arthur was not going to lose an opportunity, and when the doctor's buggy had whirled past with slightly quickened speed, he said shortly and suddenly, "Will you let me tell you what I came for?"

There was something in his tone, and still more in the expression of his face, which made Flora start violently and then turn pale, — doubtful signs; and he hurried on that there might be no misapprehension of his meaning: "You must know, you must have seen, how much I love you."

"Oh, no! I never dreamed of such a thing! Pray, pray, say no more about it!"

"I must speak, now that I have the chance. Don't be frightened — forgive me for being too sudden — only listen to me."

"No, please do not. It will only make it worse."

"Make what worse? Surely you do not love — you cannot have promised yourself to anybody else?"

"No, I have not."

"Forgive me if I have been too abrupt; but it seems to me as if a man cannot love a woman as much as I love you, without her knowing it."

"I never dreamed of such a thing," repeated Flora, apologetically.

"I do love you, with all the power there is in me."

"Don't say such things; you ought not, indeed you ought not."

"Why not? — because you don't love me? I don't ask it — yet. Dearest, only be willing to let me love you, and I will make you so happy that you can't help it. Only say you will be my wife, and I will take care of all that." He paused, anxiously looking for some sign of yielding, but there was no emotion visible in the beautiful lines of her profile as she looked straight before her with downcast eyes.

"You don't dislike me — do you?"

"No."

"Don't you like me — a little?"

"You must not ask such questions," said Flora, suddenly turning round; "I have given you no right to do so. I could not think at first just what I ought to say, because I was so surprised; but I cannot be your wife. I am sure of that."

"But why not?"

"I do not want to."

"Why not?"

"That ought to be enough."

"Not for me; that will never do for me. There is no possibility for me of life without you. You have confessed you do not dislike me; perhaps to-morrow I can make you own to a little more. Dearest Flora, you don't know, you can't guess how I will strive to make you happy; you don't know how happy I can make you. I can give you rest and care, — you need them, — and books and music and pictures, and every delightful thing you can dream of; I can take you to your old home; I will let you have plenty to give to your sister. Can't you like me well enough to let me do all this for you?"

"You are not fair; you give me no choice. Of what use would it be for me to say I don't like you? You would not leave off asking me." She stopped, a hot red flush dyeing her cheeks and throat, and quivering painfully with her labored breath. "I will tell you the real reason. If a man says he loves a woman, he has a right to hear the truth from her. I cannot be your wife, not because I do not love you, — that need not come into the question at all; I cannot, because you do not love me."

"Flora!"

"You think you do, maybe."

"I know it. There is nothing I know so well. I loved you the first moment I saw you, though I did not know it then, — not till I went away from you. If I had known it I could not have gone. Since then I have thought of you, dreamed of you, seen you every minute. I love you better than everything else in the world; indeed, it seems to me sometimes that I have never loved anything else at all."

"You have always loved — yourself."

"That was before I had seen you."

"If you never loved any one but me, your love is not the right kind. You have worked and planned and thought, all for yourself. I know, of course, how much you have done for your family, but it was all because you thought it was proper for your own character and reputation that it should be done; it was not for their sakes. You don't love them."

"Is that wholly my fault?"

"Very likely not. I don't blame you. I have no right to do so, and I know how hard a life you have lived, and how much you have had to make you selfish; but you are — that is all. Forgive me if I say more than I ought; but I must tell you the truth, or you will not be satisfied."

"I am selfish, I own it; all men are, — but you would make me better."

"All men are *not* selfish!" burst out Flora. "Oh!" she went on, now trembling from head to foot, "you can't have a heart — you can't love — or you would love Orlando, and feel for him a little. He's the best man that ever lived. You are hardly fit to be his brother, and you treat him as if he were the ground beneath your feet. I heard all you said to him when you were here last; I did not want to, but I could not help it. And you have grown up with him from a boy! If you don't love him, you can't love anybody."

"I did consider Orlando's conduct worthy of blame. You don't understand how men look at these things."

"And you don't understand how it all happened. If you had loved him at all you would have asked for his reasons — his excuses; you would have wanted to hear them, so that you might have felt it right to do more for him." She passed her hand over her eyes, as if calling up old recollections; then, looking up, she went on with a faltering voice: "When my father died, we had so little that Aunt Esther said she and Ida would have to do something. I was only fourteen then, and she thought I was too young to teach for another year at least. Ida was seventeen, and very well fitted; but she was afraid to go anywhere alone, and Aunt wrote to one of her old friends, and got a place at Cazenovia. Ida was to teach, and I was to study, and work some for my board, and we were very glad, because we could all keep together. Orlando was just ordained and settled there, and he and Ida became engaged directly, but they did not mean to marry till they had saved a little; he wanted to have his mother live with them, and she wanted to, and he said he knew you would go on doing something for her — only, he wanted to do his share. But Aunt Esther felt very ill; she did not know what the matter was with her, but she thought if she could only hold out another year! but she could not; and then the doctor — Orlando had Dr. Griscom come from here — said it was a cancer, and could n't be cured. She kept on a little longer." Flora's eyes were now brimming with tears, which she struggled to keep back. "When Orlando found out how it was, he and Ida were married directly, so that Auntie might have a home to go to. She lived two years after that, and Ida was never well after Landy was born; and he couldn't help running into debt, though he tried, he did try, to keep out of it. He took me in too, and never breathed a word about its being a burden."

"I should think that you had more than paid for everything that Orlando has done for you."

"We never asked which gave the most," said Flora, a flash of violet light piercing her eyelashes. "People don't want to be done for — they want to be loved. Yes, I know you have done everything for your mother, but Orlando has loved her. You think you love me now, but you don't know what it really is. You want to marry me because I am pretty, or you think so; but you don't know me. If I lost that there would be nothing else in me for you to care about. I am an ignorant girl, — ignorant, at least, of what you would want your wife to know. I know nothing about society, or what is going on in the world. You would find me stupid. I saw you looking at Ida at dinner to-day, as if you wondered whether she ever looked like me. She used to be a great deal prettier, though perhaps you would not think so now; but Orlando loves her just as much as when he married her — more — now that she is pale and sickly and nervous, yes, and cross sometimes; women have to be when they have had so much pain as she has; but he has never lost his patience with her one single moment. There is nothing he would not do for her; he would die for her — I do believe he would beg for her; it could not be any worse than to bear the things you said to him. I want to be loved like that!"

"If I married you I should love like that!"

Flora shook her head. "No," she said, "I could not make you different. I am not good enough or wise enough. I should like all those things you spoke of, — rest and freedom and pretty things; and I should get drawn away from all of them here, and I could not bear it. You must not think that I speak only for myself, — I do it for your sake too. If I loved you twice as well as I do, I would not marry you. If I did, you would try to make me live your life, and see with your eyes — every man wants his wife to do that; you would try to make me go against my own sense of what was right, and we should both grow worse."

"You will drive me mad!" burst out Arthur, losing his composure. "Is happiness so common a thing in this world that we must both of us miss it on account of your over-fine scruples? They are foolish — wrong."

"There are better things than happiness. We are often unhappy here, but I can bear it. Before you came, it never seemed so hard. Please do not say anything more; go away and don't come back; you will soon get over caring for me. Try and marry some girl who will be fit for the world you live in, — some good girl who owes no duty here, and who will do you good instead of your doing her harm. What she might give them or do for them would be kindness, and not buying them off, as it would be in me."

She spoke in short breathless sentences, with a pause after each one; and now she stopped, and stood a moment, shaking so that he involuntarily put out his arm to save her from falling; but she rejected it in a way not to be mistaken, and walked on again more rapidly. Their path was bringing them back to the village square where a livelier murmur of voices and steps had begun to arise as the sun sloped toward the west and the hour hand of the town clock toward the nadir.

"Do you think that I am going to give you up like that?" said Arthur, desperately.

"Pray, don't say any more. It will be of no use, and it will only make us both unhappy."

They were crossing the green now, out of hearing of every one, if not out of sight; but he could not trust himself to speak without giving full vent to the burning tide of passion, love, or hate, he could not tell which, for this beautiful, provoking, incomprehensible creature. Was ever love confessed, or refused, in so maddening, so tantalizing a fashion? He was silent; but she looked at him with some fear in her eyes, and he did not wonder, for he felt savage enough. His ears were ringing, and his pulse throbbing with a mad desire to seize upon her — kiss her, kill her! Had there but been a desert around them! But as it was, he only opened the rickety gate for her to pass, and said in his usual courteous, deliberate tones, "Don't you think that you have been a little hard upon me?"

He scorned himself for saying it; as if that were all that could come of that tempest within! But it seemed to touch her, for she turned on the back doorsteps, and said tremulously, "I am sorry if I have. Please forgive me." They stood alone together under the now darkening back porch, hidden by its overhanging creepers. There was no bearing it. He caught her hand; but she snatched it from him with a sudden impulse of strength which he could not have overcome without using more force than the still powerful instincts of a gentleman allowed, and rushed into the house and up the stairs, leaving him baffled, angry with himself and her, raging with the desire to work his anger off, and yet perfectly at a loss how.

Go back and give her up? Never! Stay and try his fate again? Useless! She held the key of the whole situation in her hands. He could never be alone with her a moment unless she chose; and she would not choose. He now remembered, with a curse on his own folly, the little talk on business which they had had together when he was here last, and which must have been in her thoughts when she showed herself so easy of access to-day.

The thought crossed his mind for a moment of asking Orlando's good offices in the matter. Orlando, he thought, would have sense to see that the girl was uselessly sacrificing herself and her prospects, and influence enough to persuade her to listen to reason, and, Arthur felt with a quick responsive throb of the heart, her own inclinations. But that Orlando, of all men, should have such power over a woman! and one who was not in love with him, whose virgin girlish dreams (he did not allow vanity to lure him with the fancy that they could be any thing more) were full of another's image, — it was incredible!

"It shows," he thought, "how these parsons can get round the women;" and he had never used to think that Orlando made much of a figure at his own trade. No, he was not so poorly off yet that he need stoop to that. He did not doubt of ultimate success, for he had never known defeat. He would stay a few days, and wait for some signs to guide him on his path; and then, he could not go. His whole physical nature craved another sight of Flora, as the starving crave for food.

A step on the walk made him start. He had been oblivious of all his surroundings, but he now recognized the approaching form of his brother Orlando, in a long linen duster, tall and gaunt, travel-stained and weary; and starting in his turn at the unexpected appearance of his brother, he said, —

"How do you do, Orlando?"

"That you, Arthur? We did not expect you."

"No, I had business this way, and having a day or two, thought I would run out here."

This explanation seemed to clear a cloud from his brother's face. "Well, we're glad to see you; I wish things were better here."

"Never mind that now."

Orlando looked relieved again, set down his rusty leather bag on the bench, and began to unbutton his duster.

"Have you had your supper?" he asked. "They must be through now; come in and have some with me. Flora'll get something. Flora!"

"She is upstairs, I think. No, thank you,

Orlando, I won't trouble you to-night;" and he strolled back to his boarding-house, where a supper of peculiarly uninviting aspect was waiting for him. He wondered, rather grimly, how many such meals he was doomed to eat there before he succeeded in winning Miss Flora Shepherd's consent to be his. He did not give two thoughts to Orlando, who, indeed, was not giving two to him. Poor Orlando had come home disappointed as usual; but what he found there allowed him no time to dwell on anything else.

Arthur did not go to his mother's till the afternoon of the next day, recognizing the fact that the less Flora saw of him for a day or two, the better for his cause. But there was no bearing it longer, and toward sundown he set forth, telling himself that he would not take her by surprise, — he would ring the front doorbell, and give her fair warning. It would be hardly possible, if he stayed long enough, that he should not see her at least. But the front door was open wide, though no one came or went, and he walked in, and through the open door of the little parlor to where she was sitting with the baby on her lap. He had come gently, but something there was in the hush of the place that made his tread echo in his own ears, and he stopped short, before she had raised one hand ever so slightly, and his eyes had followed it as it sank slowly down again to rest, light as a dropped feather, over the baby. Her own gaze was riveted on its face, which drew his too, with a kind of fascination, even when hers was so near it. The little creature's eyes were half open, but no glimmer of light came from them; the lines around its mouth were settling sharp and rigid, as if an icy wind were sweeping over them, and a little bubble between its motionless lips quivered to show that the breath still went and came.

"I am afraid—" Arthur began in a low tone.

"Yes," said Flora, "he was taken much worse last night, just as I came home."

"Has the doctor seen him?"

"Yes; he says there is nothing to do; he cannot swallow anything. I have brought him down here, so that Ida can get some sleep. She was awake all night, and while he is in the room she wants to keep looking at him."

"Where is Orlando?"

"He has taken the other children out, to

keep the house quiet. Mrs. Butler is taking a nap." She paused, then answered his unspoken question with, "There is nothing you can do — don't wait."

"I can stay with you, at any rate," said he, sitting down beside her, his heart swelling with pity for the lonely girl, as it had done before he knew that any concern for self mingled in his emotion. Surely no self should enter here now! and yet, as he watched her bending head, he wished her his, even were that his own child in her arms. Selfish as vain the wish, he told himself.

They sat side by side in the darkened room, silently waiting while the little departing life fluttered at its open gate — lingered — passed. Still they sat long together without moving, till it seemed to him as if the cold, blue-white shadows which were deepening on the baby's face were reflected on the face that bent above it, pale too, but with a difference. The pallor of life and of death, of intense feeling and of eternal repose, as he looked, seemed to grow alike and to blend. He made an involuntary motion, which he would fain have recalled, as she too now stirred, rose, and laying her burden tenderly on the sofa, drew a handkerchief over its face.

"Will you mind staying here a little longer?" she asked; "I must meet Orlando when he comes, and tell him. He will tell Ida."

Arthur was only too glad to be asked; and he stood by her at the window, till his brother approached the house, a child in each hand, and Flora, her eyes now brimming over, met him at the door without a word.

"Poor little Flora!" said Orlando; "you have been very good to him always, dear, and you know he is at rest now." He passed on into the room, and raised the covering from his baby's face a moment, his own mouth twitching a little. "Oh, you were here?" he asked absently, as he saw his brother.

"Yes," said Arthur; "I am very glad I was, for I think it was a comfort to Miss Shepherd to have some one."

"Oh, yes; I am glad you were; it was very kind in you. Flora, poor child, it seemed as if she was bound up in him. If anything could have kept him alive she would. But it is all right for him; he is safe from the trials and temptations of this world."

"Yes," said Mrs. Butler, tearfully, as she now entered the room with Flora, "it is a lovely thing that so many dear little lambs are taken away before they know what sin and sorrow are." Mrs. Butler had progressed from the early Calvinistic belief of the damnation of non-elect infants to the more cheerful if less logical position that all babies were sure to be saved in some way. "It has always been a consoling thought," she went on, "that one third of the human race dies in infancy."

Orlando looked a little hurt at this, though he had uttered this very sentiment in a sermon; but his mother had a way of applying scraps of pulpit eloquence on inappropriate occasions.

"I must go up to Ida," he said, stopping to give Flora a consolatory kiss, and a few whispered words. Arthur took the opportunity to say, "You must let me attend to everything;" and having made a few arrangements he hurried off, Mrs. Butler aimlessly following him. Flora, left alone, could throw herself on the floor, and bury her face in her place of refuge, the baby's white nest. It was cold and still there now, but that was better than to have it empty, as it soon must be. In a moment Mrs. Butler came fussing back, and the children, left outside by their father, shouted under the window; but she was ready for them then.

Arthur had met Dr. Griscom at the gate, and stopped for a word or two with him. The doctor was a man of consequence in Liverpool, having a good house there, a farm just out of the town, and "money out at interest." He had a wide back-country practice, and was often called into consultations in Syracuse. He was tall and thin, with grizzled hair, and a kindly keen-sighted look, and in his old clothes had an air of superiority, the combined result of early education and the long autocracy which a country doctor enjoys. He was now throwing curious glances at Arthur over his spectacles, trying, as was his wont when they met, to trace some link between the barefoot boy of his old remembrances and this elegant young man, and oddly struggling between his former good-natured condescension and his present unavoidable deference to one now wonted to a wider sphere than his own. They walked, still talking, back to the house, and would have gone in; but the sight through the doorway of the lonely figure by the couch stayed them, and they turned again to the gate in silence, and ended their colloquy in subdued tones. But when the doctor had given Arthur one or two addresses, and asked one or two questions, he still lingered, and at last, throwing a quick glance at the closed blinds of the windows, said, "Flora Shepherd is a very uncommon girl."

"She seems to be so."

"I ought to know, and I say she would appear an uncommonly fine girl anywhere."

"You are right, I have no doubt."

"Any man," went on the doctor, "any *young* man, who had the very slightest chance of getting that girl for a wife, and did not try, with all his might, would be the greatest fool I know."

"I agree with you entirely," said Arthur, looking straight at the doctor before he walked off.

"Well — well!" muttered the old man to himself, rather taken aback by this sudden outburst of candor, "I am glad — yes," choking down a rising lump in his throat, "I am heartily glad of it!"

CHAPTER IX.

ARTHUR worked off his excited feelings of compassion, as men are prone to do, by spending money, and ordered everything for the baby's funeral in "real style" according to the undertaker, which meant everything as simple and as expensive as possible. He sent out from Syracuse gardens a great quantity of the rarest flowers, which Flora touched with conflicting emotions; but she could thoroughly sympathize with Ida's gratification. It was a genuine comfort to them both to think that the poor baby, whose birth had been unheralded by gifts, and whose life had been spent in the cast-off clothes of others, should have some possessions of his own at last, if only a few withering rosebuds shut up within a coffin-lid.

Orlando himself said the few short and simple words of the funeral service, very calmly, and did not, his mother thought, sufficiently improve the occasion. Ida was just able to come downstairs, pale but lovely even in her unchecked tears, which flowed feebly, keeping time, as it were, to her languid pulses. She did not attempt to go with the rest to the grave, but when they rose to go she held out her hand to Arthur, saying, "Thank you so much for this and all your other kindness"

We all know people whose power of comic expression resides more in voice and manner than in the words; but Ida and her sister had tones and looks that gave a calm intensity to all they said, no matter how trivial; and surely, nothing ever heightened the power of beauty more. Flora had given no direct thanks; but she consulted Arthur on all the arrangements for the occasion in a free and unconscious way, which pleased him by showing her gratitude, if it maddened him by asserting a confidence he could not betray; no avoiding him, no shrinking from him; she would come up to him wherever he might be, and with her eyes, running over with tears, full on him, talk to him as freely as to Orlando. They walked side by side in the short procession which entered the cemetery gate, and stood side by side while the tiny grave was filled, under the shadow of a plain but handsome family monument, which some of Arthur's first gains had gone to erect. On its polished surface, he now read a name which recalled the fact, almost forgotten, that another Arthur Butler had been brought here before in his babyhood, an older brother of his own, who had died before he was born. "Poor little man! your place was soon filled up!" he thought. "You had no one to love you, like — If you had, I could wish I had been you!" And he looked at Flora, who was calm and tearless now, for the John Butlers, who had brought Laurea "to see her little cousin buried," were there, and before them she would show no emotion. Almira's sharp looks at her were unheeded, and the doctor's kindlier interest, apparent to Arthur, was unnoticed by her. But when they reached the house again she stopped before going up to her sister, who had been left in charge of a Mrs. Rand, a good-hearted, loud-spoken, neighboring widow, and held out her hand. "Good-by, Mr. Butler; I suppose I shall not see you again;" and then in her sister's words and tone: "Thank you so much for all your kindness."

"I shall see you again before you go," said Orlando, following her. It seemed a foregone conclusion in the minds of the whole family that he was going as soon as possible; and indeed, what had he to wait for? Flora had given him a strong hint that it would be of no use to stay.

"Heard about Jonah?" asked John, who was loitering about waiting for his wife, who had also gone upstairs to bid good-by before her drive home.

"No, I don't remember," said Arthur, vaguely recollecting that his mother had said something when he first arrived. "I hope he is doing well."

"So-so; he's got a place with Hewson, a man who farms it out Fabius way; but I guess he gets pretty poor pay; and I've been wonderin' why he don't turn up here again. Hewson's a Baptist, and a professor, but he's a regular screw."

"You shouldn't talk against church-members, John," said his mother.

"I've traded with him," said John.

"I am glad, at any rate," said Mrs. Butler, "that Mr. Hewson is a professing Christian. I have a great respect for the Baptists, though I see no Scriptural grounds against infant baptism, — you were all christened; but if Jonah wanted to be immersed, I should not mind it at all."

"He'll be in deep enough before he gets through," said John, winking. "There's a girl at the Hewsons', though she's an old one; she'll get him in if Father Hewson don't."

"I hope she is pious," said Mrs. Butler, wiping her eyes. "I think a pious wife might do a good deal for Jonah; I did hope before he left he had some serious thoughts; he had several very bad nights, which is often a sign of being under conviction; but it turned out that it was only the pies; Flora had made the crust very heavy that week."

"You mustn't be sayin' anythin' against Florer, mother," said John; "it ain't fair to tell the men that a girl can't make good pie-crust — hey, Arthur?"

"I should never think of saying anything against dear little Flora," said Mrs. Butler. "She is a good Christian girl if ever there was one, and I should be only too glad if dear Jonah would take a fancy to her. I always hoped he would, living in the same house, and everything. But he thinks far too much of outward attractions; he says she does not carry style enough for him; I wish that Jonah —"

"Oh, damn Jonah!" interrupted Arthur, but without the least hint of irritation in his utterance, slow and polished as ever, so that his mother at first doubted whether she heard aright, and then remained speechless with horror, while John, on the contrary, "snatched a fearful joy" mingled with a sudden reinforcement of respect for his brother. Mrs. Butler had always thought her second son's salvation problematical, and from that time she regarded his perdition as almost inevitable. She took herself out of the room, with a frightened expression, as soon as the John Butlers had driven off, leaving Orlando alone with him, as if for purposes of exorcism. But Orlando could only begin mildly with: "Thank you, Arthur; you have been very good. I am sorry to have caused you all this additional expense."

"That was a gift — don't mention it. I was very glad to be able to do it."

"I hoped I should not be a burden on you much longer, but the position in the Geneseo Academy, for which I have been applying, has been given to somebody else.

There are always so many after such a place."

Orlando in his best funereal array looked threadbare enough, more like the "usher" dear to fiction, than one likely to find favor in a "growing academy." But Arthur, as he turned to go, answered absently, "Never mind; there will be other things probably."

"If you should come across anything within my powers — some secretaryship, or some such thing; I can write fast and legibly — "

"I cannot say. I know of nothing at present," said Arthur, who particularly disliked holding out expectations to his family; they were ready enough, he thought, to form them without encouragement. "Good-by, Orlando. I am sorry to hurry, but I shall miss my train."

Orlando looked wistfully after him, wishing he had spoken a little sooner, when Arthur had a little more time, and when he might have had a better chance of explaining his wishes and capabilities; and feeling, too, that he ought to have expressed more gratitude; but somehow his brother was a hard person to thank.

Arthur went back. The city, divested of pleasures, was full of work as ever, — fuller;

and he pushed on unsparingly. He could not bear stopping to think. He was toiling on for Flora's sake, but she seemed so far away that no effort could bring her nearer day by day. She must consent; but he could never fancy her doing it. When he did see her, in sleeping or waking dreams, it was always bending over the dead baby in her arms, and the shadow of death stealing over her, and then he would awake with an icy shiver at his heart; what if she should die before he saw her again? He never put so much labor into his most difficult case as he now spent in trying to find some situation for Orlando. The one he had been offered was now filled, and it was likely to be some time before he could lay any one else who had an easy berth for a retired indigent minister at his disposal under sufficient obligations to obtain the filling of it. But he was sure of one in time. Orlando must come to Boston and bring his whole family with him, including Flora of course; and when he had her where he could see her daily, no one else should have the very smallest chance, — he was sure of that; and that granted, time must work on his side. How long would it be before she could forget that she had refused to be "bought off" by him, when every fresh kindness he did for his family would remind her of it? It must be long; for himself he doubted if he could ever forget it; but he thought he had enough magnanimity never to reproach her with it after she had changed her opinion.

In the second week in September, after a day largely spent in inquiries on his brother's behalf, crowded in upon a hundred other matters, the sight of a little note in a well-remembered handwriting, gave him a sense of pre-existence. It only said: —

900 *Marlborough Street*, BOSTON,
September 14, 188–.

MY DEAR MR. BUTLER, — I am sorry that I have not had the pleasure of seeing more of you this summer; but we are both of us such busy people that it seemed impossible to arrange it. I have come to town earlier than usual for a few days, because I have rather suddenly made up my mind to go abroad this fall. My cousin Sophy accompanies me, and we stay a year, or perhaps eighteen months. I hope I may have an opportunity to wish you good-by; can you not come and dine with me to-morrow, or any day this week? — quite by ourselves, at seven o'clock.

Yours very sincerely,
RACHEL TOWNSEND CURTIS.

Arthur thought over all his talks with Miss Curtis, in which they had planned a foreign tour. He had never gone, and she often had, until, as she declared, she was weary of travelling, and would not go again, unless she had the excitement of taking a fresh observer with her. If he could manage to run over for a few months, she really did not know but she might go too, and take some of the girls. Frances had never been yet; and then Sophy was asked if she would not like to go again, and had blushed as she replied that she would like to very much, with a pleasant party. But latterly the subject had been dropped, — Miss Curtis and Arthur tacitly agreeing that it would not do to bring it up till Sophy and he were openly engaged. It was painful to recall all this alone, and it would be more painful still to recall it together, but it was a pain that could not be shirked, and he wrote on the spot, and accepted for the morrow.

That little party of three — how like old times, and yet how unlike, it seemed to them all! They talked on the old subjects, after their first meeting had been as skilfully got through as was in the power of high breeding to accomplish; but still their talk would languish, and their attention flag. Miss Curtis, in spite of herself, had hoped something from the occasion. Meeting again after an interval does sometimes clear up misunderstandings. She had debated whether to ask a fourth or not; it might be more awkward to have one, and it might be less. She had vacillated — asked one man who could not come; had been glad of it, and now felt regretful, and wished some one would drop in; but no one did. All these perplexities assailed her, while her tongue glibly reeled off small talk, — going straight to Scotland — not too late — just the right time — stay with the Rantouls — they have taken the house on Oronsay — yachting in the Western Islands — Staffa — Iona — always wanted to see them — Culdees — crosses — cromlechs — Collins' Ode. She was wondering, meanwhile, if the others were racking their brains as she was, while the clock musically mocked her distress as every quarter came round.

At nine o'clock there came a welcome break, as the butler brought in a note with, "The man wishes to know if there is any answer, ma'am?"

Miss Curtis read the note once; she read

it twice; she read it thrice. It was from her next neighbor but one, who was also passing through town for a few days, on a very trivial matter, and the simplest verbal message would have sufficed for an answer; but in the time which it gave her for thought, she formed a plan for one last effort. Perhaps a few minutes' *tête-à-tête* might even now explain the whole; and while she read the note the fourth time she made up her mind, with some shame at her plotting, which she set aside as her own sacrifice, that no one else need ever know.

"Tell the man, please, to say to Mrs. Montgomery that I will come in in a moment. Excuse my leaving you," to the young people; "but I find I must see Mrs. Montgomery about this; I shall not be long — not more than half-an-hour; and you," to Arthur, "will wait till I come back. It is early yet."

"Cannot I see Mrs. Montgomery for you, and save you the trouble?" said Arthur, with unpromising readiness.

"Oh no, that would be impossible — no, no, don't disturb yourself — don't get up;" and she hurried out of the room as quickly as she could, unheeding Sophy's look of pleading expostulation, strong as the girl dared to make it, and thought she had done it, on the whole, very naturally.

In the half-hour which followed, Arthur Butler expiated some of his sins, and recognizing the fact, made no complaint of Fortune or of his old friend. He felt that he deserved that the punishment should be even worse than it was; that it was not was due to Sophy, who gallantly sustained the credit of her sex. The longer the time grew, (and Miss Curtis, now that she was "in for it," made it long), the more unflagging was her flow of talk, skimming the surface like a smooth pebble, without ever once ruffling the depths. They talked gossip and guide-books, though the one topic was stupid and the other loathsome. What did Sophy care for the old world, so often traversed by her, and in which she was now to look for some new distraction in untrodden ways? What did Arthur care for anything in nature or in art that he had once longed for? Only to know if a girl in a little town which he knew through and through, and on which he had so often gladly turned his back, was thinking of him ever — then — just then. As they both began to feel that they could not stand it much longer, Miss Curtis came back, and Arthur rose.

"I think I must go now, Miss Curtis," he said, sadly and quietly. "I have some work on hand for the evening, and I ought not to keep you up late; you must have a great deal to see to, — cannot I help you in any way?"

"No, thank you. Really there is nothing to be done. I have lent this house to Mrs. Tom Wilson and her daughter; they will come in a fortnight or so."

"Good-night, then; I wish you a pleasant journey and safe return. Good-by, Miss Sophy," taking a hand of each in his; then in a still lower tone: "Thank you for all your great kindness to me; good-by!"

He knew that he had turned a page in his life at which there was no looking back, and seeing himself, as he had long been in the habit of doing, through Miss Curtis's eyes, he thought he cut but a mean figure there. Had it only been she with whom he was alone, he perhaps could have told her everything, and she, perhaps, might have forgiven; but it was too late for that.

"If Flora knew all this!" he thought, "she would certainly never have me; nay, she would probably insist on my proposing to Sophy at once;" and he could hear her doing so, in the simple way in which young girls will tell a man to do the impossible. He had a desperate feeling that he should like her to know, — that he wanted to win her with every disadvantage against him known to the bottom, and not a secret to fear the look in her eyes. He had always known that if Sophy were his wife there must be a great region of his life which she could never enter; and it had not troubled him. But with Flora the idea was unbearable. This secret, nevertheless, he must keep for Sophy's sake; and after all, Flora would have a husband in whose past there was much less worthy of blame than in that of most of the men he knew. Indeed, in the light of sober reason, he did not see that he was to blame at all; but Conscience, as is sometimes her wont, would not listen to reason.

CHAPTER X.

FROM ARTHUR BUTLER TO ORLANDO BUTLER.

Ames Building, BOSTON, MASS.,
Sept. 20, 188-.

MY DEAR ORLANDO, — Mr. Marcus Spear, the President of the Colonial-Historical Society, has at his disposal the place of Assistant Secretary, and as he is under obligations of a business nature to me, I was able to obtain the offer of it for you. The duties are, I think, within your powers, — hours from nine to five, and salary $800 a year. This will not be a very large sum on which to support your family near Boston, but you can have a room at my lodgings for the present, and they can remain in Liverpool with mother. I do not think it best that she should remove here till I can get the house there off my hands; but when I can, without too much loss, sell or lease it, you can take one in the suburbs here somewhere, and I will pay you for her board at a fair rate, and make her an allowance for her personal expenses, if you can undertake to make her comfortable. I have no doubt she will be willing to consent to this plan. I will settle your debts at Pompey and set you free with the world again, and you certainly ought to be able to keep so. I enclose a check for your travelling expenses; please get yourself a respectable suit of clothes, and come at once. Give my love to mother, and remember me to your wife and Miss Shepherd. Let me hear from you by return post, and believe me

Very sincerely yours,

ARTHUR BUTLER.

FROM ORLANDO BUTLER TO ARTHUR BUTLER.

LIVERPOOL, N. Y.,
Sept 22, 188–.

MY DEAR BROTHER,— Your most kind letter of the 20th is just received, and I cannot tell you what a relief it gives to my mind. I hope some day I may be able to defray part of the pecuniary obligation, but that of your kindness I shall never be able to. I accept the offer of the situation with gratitude. Mother will have no objection to leave Liverpool, and will enjoy being located near you. She only wishes to be in the neighborhood of some Evangelical church where Scriptural truths are really professed and taught.

Ida joins with me in fervent thanks, and seems to enjoy the idea of removing eastward, though of course it will be very different there from her own old home. But I doubt not the change will be beneficial to her. Flora, much to my surprise, does not seem to take to the project, and even said something about staying in this neighborhood, and getting a teacher's place. Of course, Ida would not hear of that, nor I either, for we could not spare her; and I think she must see that, and will not object to give up her own wishes, and accompany us. I don't know what her reasons are, but I hope she has had no thoughts of Jonah, as mother has sometimes been inclined to suspect. Though Jonah is my brother, and I wish him a good wife, yet I must say I cannot think him worthy of Flora, whom I have always regarded as the very best girl in the world, next to my own wife. John seems to think he is paying attentions to another young lady; so it will be much the best plan for her to accompany us. If Ida and the children are well, I hope she can get time to attend some good school for a term or two. Her father taught her very carefully while he lived, and I always felt that she ought to have more advantages in that way.

I cannot be in Boston on Monday morning without travelling on the Sabbath, which I have never done; and I hope you will not mind if I feel that I cannot conscientiously break my rule for any emergency if I look to being prospered in my new position. I will leave in the Monday morning train and be in Boston that evening. Mother and Ida both send love, and we all pray that the Lord will reward you with all spiritual blessing through Christ Jesus.

Ever gratefully your brother,
ORLANDO BUTLER.

Monday evening came, but Orlando had not appeared in Beacon Street. Tuesday morning — still he did not come; and Arthur, after waiting for him for some time sat down to write a note to leave for him in no very good humor. "I might have known it!" he thought. "Catch Orlando being in time, even when his living depends on it! He will find unpunctuality tell more against him than Sunday travelling there, I fancy." He went on to save time by writing a note of apology to Mr. Spear for his brother's non-appearance, in case the appointed hour came without him. It was pouring a heavy autumn rain outside, in consequence of which, perhaps, the boy was late with the newspaper, the want of which still further irritated him. It came as he finished his last note, and as it was brought in, he saw from the window the urchin who had brought it pattering across the street without any umbrella, like a vision of his own boyhood. It haunted him as he threw himself back in his comfortable study chair, and unfolded the damp sheet. On the first page blazed in the largest of type: —

DEATH ON THE RAIL!

FRIGHTFUL ACCIDENT!

LOSS OF LIFE!

TELESCOPING OF TWO TRAINS ON THE NEW YORK CENTRAL AT LITTLE FALLS.

THROUGH CAR FOR BOSTON BURNED.

TWO CLERGYMEN AND A NOTED ACTOR AMONG THE LOST.

His eye ran along these lines without taking in the closely printed text with which they were interspersed, — there was no more needed; and when he came to the second name in the list of killed, —

BUTLER, REV. ORLANDO, of Liverpool,

it seemed as if he had known years ago that this must happen, — as if his own folly must have been in some way to blame that he had not somehow warned — prevented; while, side by side with the old unreasoning protest against destiny in the past, the other half of his nature was as ready as ever to fight it in the future. Two days' work must be crowded into one before he took the night train which would rush over the field of death; and it was all done, without a detail being overlooked or forgotten.

On Wednesday afternoon John Butler was making a short visit of inspection to his China Parlors, hearing the reports of his subordinates, and issuing his orders, with a comprehensive decision as like his brother's as his more limited sphere would allow. He started as his office door opened, though the visitor was expected.

"My stars, Arthur! you do look done up, and no mistake. Sit down, won't you?" But Arthur remained standing. "I shouldn't think you'd had any sleep for a week!" and then, apologetically: "I thought there wa'n't no need of my goin' s' long as you were there, you know."

A shake of the head was the only reply.

"You got him here, I s'pose?" said John, lowering his voice.

Arthur silently assented.

"Much disfigured, was he, poor fellow?" and as Arthur grew, if possible, a shade whiter: "You don't say so! Well — poor Land was fit to go that way if it came to that, fitter than either you or I, the Lord knows!"

Arthur poured out a glass of water with a shaking hand, and slowly swallowed it.

"Goin' to Liverpool this afternoon? Want me to come with you?" went on John, whose voice sounded like the buzzing of some far-away indistinct gnat in his brother's ears.

"No — thank you. I would rather go alone."

"Well, I was there better part of yesterday, to be sure; and 't ain't very convenient to go there every day. You tell 'em I 'll be out early to-morrow; you 'll hardly have the funeral till the day after?"

"Did you tell them about it?"

"No — no — I could n't quite get myself up to that point. Almirer said she would; but I thought Ider and Florer would n't like that; they never hitched their horses with her; so I went and got Dr. Griscom; he 's accustomed to that sort of thing. He told Florer, I s'pose, and then they told the rest;" then, with another sudden lowering of his voice as he realized afresh that his tones did not befit the occasion: "I am sorry enough for Ider, poor thing. I don't see what in the land she 's to do."

"I shall take care of that."

"O—h—h!" said John, who had meant his remark to be the preface to an offer to do something, and who felt that in his impulse of real pity and regret for his brother, and out of Almira's presence, he might have gone farther than strict prudence would dictate. Still, he could hardly do nothing, and he went on: "I've told Almirer to get them their mournin' suits, Florer and all of 'em, and I'll pay the bill. She'll bring out the things to-morrow, to try 'em on. Then you really don't want me to-day?"

Arthur was only too glad to get away alone for the remainder of his weary journey; alone, but for that terrible companion, shut out forever from human sight, whose presence, though unseen, struck awe and silence into the busy crowd along the way, of which every mile grew harder as they drew nearer home. Arthur had long given up speaking, or even thinking, of Liverpool as home; his home was in the future, a future uncolored by tender reflections of the past, which only lived for him in claims of duty that he paid, as he thought, to the uttermost farthing. But what few affectionate remembrances of his boyhood he still dwelt on with pleasure were connected with his brother Orlando, his nearest in age; and his sleepless hours on the road had been haunted by pictures, almost forgotten till then, of

Orlando and himself getting together, after having been bullied and hectored by John, with the whispered resentment which is all that juniors in such a plight dare as a rule venture upon; indeed, poor little Orlando, but for the promptings of his own more daring spirit, would hardly have ventured upon that. Memory, too, was true in painting himself as domineering and overbearing; for though Mrs. Butler had been wont to assert with satisfaction that "Arthur and Orlando always agreed," Arthur knew very well on which side the agreement had been; and the recollection of a headless wooden horse, Orlando's only lawful possession in the plaything line, appropriated by Arthur because he could better harness it to its cart, brought more of a sting than that of harsh words or cold neglects of later years. He might have known, even then, that this was sure to come!

He had gone over the particulars of this and other such childish scenes, not sparing himself one detail, with a feeling that he must get the very worst. He had shed no tears,—he did not believe he ever should; they were not in his way, and this was no time for them; but when, for the third time,

Flora, though he had hoped she would not, opened the door they came fast enough, and he found himself trying to speak — choking — struggling — and then, he hardly knew how, he was on a chair in the parlor, with his head on the cold marble of the rickety centre table, shaking it all over with his violent, long-drawn sobs. They seemed to him to come from some one else, and he was conscious of surprise that they gave him any relief; but as he became aware that they were really his own, a sense of shame made him strive again for composure, then break down again hopelessly, the first gush of relief giving place to overpowering dizzy weakness.

"Arthur — dear Arthur — don't, please don't!" The words were in Flora's voice, and she was bending over him, the loose tendrils of her hair touching his neck. "Dearest Arthur!" and now she was kneeling by him, her cheek wet with both their tears. "Don't, don't feel it so terribly! You made him happy, very happy, indeed you did; I have never known him happier than he was when he got your letter;" and now the light touch of her hand was on his head, and her words died away into the tender inarticulate murmur with which she might have soothed one of the children.

"Did you read it?" he managed at last to get out with a gasping breath.

"Yes, but never mind that, — he did not. He said he did not wonder that you were a little impatient with him sometimes, and he knew you meant to be kind; and you did mean to be — did not you?"

"I — I don't know."

"I saw why you could not say any more; of course he did not know; but he thought you meant it just as well, and he knows it now. Do — do be comforted; there is so much you can do for him still!"

"He — will be here soon. Do they know? What would they —"

"You had better see them first, if you think you can; but wait a moment."

She left the room, and Arthur, recovering himself a little, and ashamed to ask by his weakness for the heaven of her touch to be continued, rose and walked with uncertain step across the floor; but she was back again in a moment with a tray in her hands. "You must have some tea, and something to eat. Yes — please do; you will feel better after it."

He could not let her stand by him and hold the cup, and took it from her hand listlessly, but not refusing, under her eyes, to drink what was in it, nor even to swallow a little food, and did feel the better for it, before his mother came in with a tearful welcome. Mrs. Butler's griefs were never too deep for tears, or words either, and her talk, apt to be a little confused, was now divided among sorrow for her son's loss, satisfaction at his sure prospects in another world, hopes that Arthur would take warning, and think of his own extremely unpromising ones, and gratitude to Heaven that he was so well able to take care of them all. Gratitude to himself, as usual, was deemed superfluous, and more thanks were bestowed on John, for the promise of the "mourning suits," than on Arthur for his intention, taken for granted, of assuming the whole care and support of his brother's widow and children. He let it pass, and avoided looking at Flora, though he could see with half an eye her cheeks flush faintly; and her "Will you not go up to see Ida?" was asked in a trembling voice.

Ida was extended on her sofa, her arm around her little girl, and her boy leaning against her shoulder, both children awed for once into quietness. She seemed hardly conscious of anything that was going on, but when Arthur came near her, she held out her little cold hand in a mechanical way, as if it were a lesson she had learned. He took it, and still holding it, sat down by her, while the children, relieved by the interruption, hung about him.

"I want you to know, Ida, that henceforth these children are mine."

"Thank you," murmured Ida, in so low a tone that he could hardly catch the words; "I am sure you will; you were always kind." She closed her eyes, and he waited a moment before he laid her hand gently down, and led away the children, who were glad to follow him into the light. There was something in her indifference to all but her grief, and her simple acceptance of his protection, that suited him better than thanks could have done.

The house was soon full of the usual subdued bustle, — surging even to the very threshold of the chamber of death, and only sparing Ida's room. How Flora contrived to keep even Almira, with her mourning and her patterns out of that, was a marvel to Arthur, who strove silently to help her, even by taking Mrs. John Butler's complaints and cross-questions on himself, repaid by the sense of a confidence between him and Flora, which, indeed, she showed as carelessly and freely as if he were her brother. It asked but too plainly for a return in kind; and yet, had there been nothing more in that one fleeting outburst of priceless tenderness? Or was even that a sign of her perfect trust that he would not ask for more? He could not now, even if the responsibilities he was taking upon himself did not render dreams of love and marriage impossible for years. He did not have her for his companion at the funeral, it being evidently considered his right to support Ida, while Flora walked behind, a child in either hand. Ida did her best not to be troublesome to him, and wept silently behind her black veil, while she tried not to burden him with the whole weight of her slight form. Though her sister-in-law's fixed opinion to the contrary was frequently and freely expressed, Ida did not like to be sickly, and a burden; indeed, she would, if she could, have been strong and healthy. She was afraid now that she had not been as good a wife to Orlando as she ought to have been; that perhaps she had not managed even as well as she might; and as she stood looking into his open grave she strove hard to remember the times — and there were a few — when he had seemed happy and hopeful. To both sisters at once vividly recurred the parting on that early Monday morning, when Flora packed his bag, and they had hoped that Arthur would think the new suit good enough.

"Arthur always looks so very elegant, does n't he?" Ida had said.

"Yes," said Flora.

"I never saw any one quite like him, did you?"

"No — but Orlando looks as nice as any one need to," Flora had replied, while at the same time she held her head low down over the open bag to hide a conscious blush, too honest to disguise from herself that everything about Arthur, even the way in which his necktie was put on, was dear to her, and ashamed that it should be so. Orlando was the best man in the world, and it would be better for Arthur if he were more like him; that she allowed, — but yet, if in changing he were to lose anything of the outward graces which had struck her foolish eyes when she first set them on him, she was not sure that she could wish it sincerely. This was what came back to her now, as she stood behind him. "Ida," she thought, as she watched her sister's drooping head, "is not so utterly unhappy. Her earthly love is fixed on heaven too, but mine — no, it was best, much the best, that I answered him as I did. Just think, if I had said yes, and then had found him unable to do all he ought for Ida; or unwilling — ever so little — and I had seen it!"

CHAPTER XI.

THE funeral was over, and the family, assembled for a few moments at their mother's house, exchanged questions and remarks on one another's several affairs, as is the custom when the scattered branches are brought together for feasting or mourning.

"When do you go back, Art? S'pose you're in a hurry, as usual?" inquired the eldest brother.

"I cannot tell to-night. I shall wait a few days, and see what Ida's wishes are."

"When be you goin', Jonah?" went on John, a little put down by Arthur's manner.

"I ain't partickler, but I guess I'll get off to-night."

"Seems to me you're in a mighty hurry to get back to old Hewson's."

Jonah snickered consciously, and looked at Arthur, who took no notice but to say, "If you mean to catch the train, you had certainly better go directly."

"Jone wanted you to plague him a bit about Miss Carrie, I guess," said John, when Jonah had finally shambled off to bid good-by to his mother.

"Why, does he mean to marry her?"

"I guess she means to marry him; it's a pretty sure thing, for she ain't got no time to waste, and Jone has. I guess he wants you to come down a little on the occasion."

"If Jonah is to be married, and tells me so in a proper way, I shall be very glad to make him a suitable present; but I really cannot be expected to divine the reasons of his behavior. You can let me know when anything definite is settled;" and he walked off to avoid a second farewell scene with Jonah, for which he saw no occasion. It was not possible to walk very far in the Butler house, and he only succeeded in getting as far as the back porch, where he sat down in a mood of disgust with himself and his surroundings. He did not like to feel that his home annoyances had the power to affect him so much, and he missed Orlando, who, though with but little of dominant character, had acted as a solvent to the irreconcilable family elements, now bidding fair to harden into utter separation, just as

Arthur felt that he craved some point of sympathy. Life looked blank and barren before him; but he had something to work for still, and that was something to live for.

Something to live for! How the hot blood surged through his pulses, and life with a flash grew beautiful, if not clear; full of doubts and difficulties, but full of hopes and promises; as Flora came out from the kitchen door in the dingiest of her old calico gowns, having slipped off her mourning, and run down to put on the kettle for an early tea for Jonah. She sat down on the bench by his side with an accustomed air, and a looker-on would have supposed that they were "courting" at the kitchen door, much as Jonah and Miss Hewson doubtless transacted their affairs. "I have been waiting to see you," he began, after she had sat a few moments, silent, sad, and calm, awaiting his pleasure. "I am afraid I shall have to leave here to-morrow, and I want to arrange some plans with your sister before I go. Perhaps I had better get your opinion of them first. I want Ida to look to me for everything, and to feel that I will do my very best for her children; she knows that."

"I am sure she does."

"But I cannot do that to my own satisfaction unless I have them somewhat nearer me."

"No."

"I shall probably be less and less able to come here."

"Yes."

"How do you think she would like to come to Boston, — I mean, just out of Boston? There is a little house in Newton that I was thinking of for them. It was bought in cheap by a man I know on a mortgage, and I can take it for a couple of years, with the privilege of buying at any time; it is in a pleasant situation, and I should think very healthy."

No answer.

"I think the sooner she goes, the better. I could have things ready for her in less than a month, and I hope by that time she will be able to come. Don't you think the change will be good for her in any case?"

"Yes, I do," said Flora, slowly but unhesitatingly.

"I do not, as I wrote Orlando, think it wise to break up here all at once, but if I can in time dispose of this house, I think it will be much better for my mother to come too, — if you are sure that she and Ida will be happy together in the same household. I want you to tell me the exact truth. I know you will."

"I think they would be very happy. They were always fond of each other."

"My mother has peculiar ways of looking at — some things; a little different, I should think, from you and your sister."

"Oh, that does n't matter. If we only do just as Mrs. Butler wants in one or two ways, she is perfectly satisfied with us; and those are no great trouble. Ida would a great deal rather have her than not."

"I am very glad."

"It will be just as well, perhaps, for her to have a little rest here by herself. Mrs. Rand will be glad to come and keep house for her, and Mrs. Butler likes her."

"That will be a very good thing; then you will have no trouble about leaving as soon as I can get ready?"

"No," said Flora, faintly. Her color went and came, and her hands moved uneasily in her lap. He himself felt the blood rush to his face as he said, careful to look away from her meanwhile, "You will go with your sister, will you not?"

"No, I cannot."

"How can she live without you?"

"She must. I know it will be hard for her, but she needs you the most; you can do so much more for her than I can."

"She might have you too."

Flora shook her head; was silent for a moment, and then said with an effort: "She and the children have a claim on you for your brother's sake. I have none."

"You have never forgiven me, then?"

"There is no question of that. I have nothing to forgive, but I don't want to live in your house any longer. I ought not."

A thin wall of ice seemed to rise between them, through which she glimmered, remote, though so near. Could he thaw it? He could not even try. He waited a minute, and then said, almost humbly, "What do you want to do?"

"I want to earn my own living. I could have done it before, but I never felt free to leave them; perhaps I ought, but I never thought," her voice faltered — "I never wanted to feel free before, but now I do.

I have known what it is to feel bound." She threw back her head, drawing a long breath, but shivering, like one who breathes the rarefied air of freedom on the heights for the first time, and finds it cold; then, with a sudden practical turn: "Dr. Griscom will help me to get a school somewhere about here for the fall term; he always said he could any time. I don't expect much at first; but I could study between, and fit for a better place next year."

"You ought not to dream of such a thing! It is not safe for you to be alone in some out-of-the-way country hole," said Arthur, regarding her with a look of annoyance, for once uncontrolled; but she returned it with one of uncomprehending wonder, and even with a very faint gleam of amusement.

"Why, what could happen to me? The doctor would see that I had a good place and boarded with nice people. He knows everybody in all the villages round. There is nothing else that I could do that I should like so well."

"Could you — could not you — stay here with my mother? I mean, of course, with Mrs. Rand too; but you would be a great comfort to her in many ways, and I should feel so much easier about her—" He dared not go on.

"I cannot," she said, very low, but decidedly; "you must not ask me." She rose, and he did too, and they stood a moment, she with averted face, till suddenly turning round she put her hand into his.

"Pray, don't be displeased with me; and forgive me if I have ever said anything to you that was unkind. I am sure we are both doing what is right now. Good-by!"

He could not speak a word; but he bent over her, and pressed a long kiss on the hand he held, — exquisite in shape, like all the rest of her, but hardened by work, and just now cold as marble.

A rattling of all the smaller articles in the kitchen announced the approach of Mrs. John Butler, who had come to know "if Florer did n't ever mean to get tea. I 've been settin' with the old lady, or I 'd have seen to it myself. If I was Arthur, I 'd have taken my tea here to-night," she continued, as they gathered round the table. "I s'pose our set-out ain't good enough for him; but it looks sort of unfeelin'." Arthur had disappeared unseen before her onward advance, and gone in despair to visit Dr. Griscom, conscious that he was making himself ridiculous to that keen-sighted observer, by his entreaties to him to "look after" Flora, yet unable to help suggesting various projects which the doctor summarily pooh-poohed as chimerical. However, he promised to "write if there were anything to say," and to "do something" if there were "anything to do," and wound up the interview, as Arthur rose to go and lingered, with, "Don't lose heart and back out, that's all! Flora Shepherd is only twenty, and if you waited for her ten years you would still be a great deal luckier fellow than you deserve to be!"

"I am happy in agreeing with you again," said Arthur, as he took his leave, not dissatisfied that since the doctor must know so much, he was so correctly informed.

Flora, meanwhile, was going through a more difficult interview with her sister. That they were to be separated had never occurred to Ida for a moment, and though she saw the justice of Flora's arguments, and opposed none thereto, it was not without many tears that she finally reached the point of making definite arrangements for her journey, — Flora promising to come on at any time in spite of everything, if Ida were *very* ill, and Ida not to send unless she were very ill *indeed*. She saw Arthur for a few moments the next day before he went, and agreed resignedly and gratefully to everything he said, while Flora, standing silent behind her, noted down in her mind all the practical directions, and as soon as he was gone proceeded to carry them out with the assistance of her friend Dr. Griscom. The doctor knew of a school at Cold Spring, within driving distance, where he only had to say a word to the committee; he also promised to arrange for her taking a course in the Chautauqua Home Studies, and to drive over on Sundays to see her sometimes. He went to Boston with Ida and the children, — a step that amazed all Liverpool, and made Mrs. John say that "if Florer didn't look out, Ider would get ahead of her." However, as soon as he returned he drove Flora over to Cold Spring to begin her duties, with her little trunk strapped on behind, — patting her on the head as he bade her good-by, and telling her to be a good child, and it would all come out right, in a way that was soothing to her, though it might have exasperated Arthur had he been by to see, and took his lonely homeward way, unable, in his secret soul, to help a subdued satisfaction in the thought that it would probably be some time coming out right, and that he had a fair number of Sunday drives to which to look forward.

CHAPTER XII.

FROM IDA TO FLORA.

NEWTON CENTRE, MASS.
May 3, 188-.

MY OWN DARLING FLORA, — It does not seem possible that it is seven whole months to-day since the day I left Liverpool — dear, blessed place! — and you, my dearest, and took that long, dreadful journey without you; but it is. I have thought of it as every month came round. I long for you more to-day than any of the others, it is so lovely here now, and you would enjoy it so much. You don't know what splendid places there are all around us, and they are all full of flowers now. My own little garden is as pretty as can be, for Arthur has taken great pains with it; he had a great many bulbs set out last fall, and they have been too beautiful. The hyacinths and tulips are in full bloom now, and there are a great many flowering shrubs. Since you wrote to me about all you were studying, I wanted to study something, too, and Miss Meade is giving me and the children lessons in botany together. She knows so much about everything! — I should think almost too much to teach such little children, but Arthur says they ought to have a lady and a thoroughly educated one about them now, even more than later. I am afraid he gives her a great deal, for she is worth it. She does make them behave so nicely; and then Arthur himself does so much good to Landy, — he is making a perfect little gentleman of him, just what his father always longed to see him. If he only could!

I do so long to show them both to you, dearest, and wish sometimes that I could truly say that I was ill enough to send for you; but I ought not to want such a thing, and I really am very well indeed, and so much stronger. I told you last week that Katy had gone, and that I was going to try to get along with only Lizzie and a woman to wash by the day, and I find it answers perfectly well, though Arthur was very much afraid it would not, and wanted me to get some one else directly. But I really like all the exercise it gives me to do part of the work, and Lizzie is quite contented, for she could never get along with Katy. I could not bear to have Arthur spending so much of his money upon us, though he says I do with wonderfully little. He ought to be thinking of marrying himself, for how happy he would make some nice girl, if he only finds one good enough for him.

On Saturday Mrs. McCall asked the children to a little party at her house; only a very few for the afternoon, and tea. I asked Arthur if I had better let them go, — they wanted to so much, — and he approved of it, and said the McCalls were very respectable people. It was Miss Meade's half-holiday, and I hated to keep her all day just for that, so I sent Lizzie with them, and she left them there, and I went for them myself a little while before it was time to come home. I dreaded it, for you know I have been nowhere but to church since I came here, but Mrs. McCall has been so kind to me that I thought I ought to; so I mustered up all the courage I could, though I stood a quarter of an hour at the gate before I could make up my mind to go in. Oh, how I did long for you! I should not have minded it if we had been together; but I did go in at last, and was glad I did, for I really enjoyed it, after the first shock of meeting so many was over. There were not many grown-up people there, and they were all so kind. Mrs. Lamson and Mrs. Searle were there, who, you will remember, I told you had called on me. As for Mrs. McCall, she is perfectly delightful, just as if she were my mother. She begged me to come again, and said I need not call it visiting, but she wished I would bring Landy and Flossy and let them play about her beautiful grounds. They are far more lovely inside than seen from without, and the house is magnificent.

I do think our children were the prettiest there; and they behaved so nicely! I wish you could have seen them. Landy wore the sailor suit I made for him. I had his old bought one for a pattern; but Arthur was surprised I could do so well. I told him I was nothing to you in such ways. As for Flossy, she wore her white frock that I wrote you about. Every one did admire her hair so; and Landy's, since his was cut, curls in rings all over his head, so that I am quite reconciled to having it short, though I hated the idea, and only had it done because Arthur said he was getting too old for long hair.

Dearest, dearest Flora, I feel like only part of myself without you. Of course, I miss dear Orlando every moment, and sometimes I feel it to be almost too hard that he could not have been spared to see us so much better off; but I know he is happier now than he could be even here. But I cannot bear to think of your being all alone by yourself in Cold Spring. Don't you think you might find some teaching here? I don't see why you should object to teaching Landy and Flossy; only, I should not like to give up Miss Meade, on her own account, for she says she likes the place better than any she ever had. She seems very fond of me and the children, and admires Arthur intensely. She thinks him the finest man she ever saw. I shall consult him, and see if he cannot think of some plan for getting you here; I am sure he will. I shall tell him I can't live without you any longer. I see him now coming from the station before lunch, which is unusual, and he seldom comes out on Mondays, anyhow; so I must close this with fondest love from

Your own IDA.

P. S. Arthur has come for me to go into town with him to choose a wedding present for Jonah.

I dare say before you get this you will have heard that he is married to Carrie Hewson. They did not write till it was over, and Arthur only heard this morning. I hope she is a good girl, and will please dear mother. Do find out all you can about her, and let me know.

   Miss FLORA M. SHEPHERD,
      Care of Mr. Martin Van Slyck,
         Cold Spring, New York.

Flora opened and read this letter in her room, some nine feet square, at Cold Spring. It held but little furniture, and what there was, was cheap and well-worn, but it was in the nicest and most precise order. As the occupant did her own washing, she could afford cleanliness as well, and the white draperies, the only sign of luxury, were spotless, if scant and none too fine. The place had somewhat the effect of a convent cell, and Flora, in her straight, plain black gown, which, though not new, had the effect of being as dazzlingly fresh in black as her surroundings in white, might have sat for the nun but for the indefinite air of promise, that had not yet, even in sadness, left her youthful face. She read the letter over again and again, with careful study. Ida was evidently recovering the tone of her mind, and taking a little comfort in what remained, — that was well. Arthur was evidently doing all he could for Ida and the children, and that he could do so much was well too, though it made her own hope of being able to help them a much more distant one. She wondered how much he spent on them a year, and she took out her own small savings'-bank book, though she knew without looking how much she had already put by. It was her dream to lay up a respectable sum, until she could feel justified in applying for a place near Boston, — a good place with a good salary; and she felt that such a one might be within her reach, with all the time and thought she was putting into hard study, — so that she might offer to contribute half of Ida's and the children's expenses. It was not fair to Arthur Butler, she reasoned, that if she would not have him he should be deprived of the chance of marrying some one else if he wanted to; and if he did not want to marry any one else — and Flora, though she always felt ashamed, and tried to hurry over this latter supposition, had a secret consciousness that he would not — it might be well to have something of her own too.

This was a very nice little plan, the only objection to it being that it required for its execution at least double the time that the doctor had mentioned as the limit of waiting. But to Flora, whose ideas of money values were on a very small scale, and who had not the faintest conception of how much Arthur made or spent in a year, it seemed most promising. She found her chief happiness in thinking it over, and congratulated herself on getting a vacation school for small children whose mothers wished to be rid of their presence for part of the day through the heats of summer; the gain was small, but every little would help. Sustained by hope, she did not heed that her sister's letters grew, as summer advanced, shorter and more irregular. She supposed Ida was busy, and was glad she should be, — it was best for her. Her good neighbors, the McCalls, she wrote, were going to the Isles of Shoals for the month of August, and wanted her and the children to go with them; and Arthur insisted that she should, it would be so good for them all, — and take Lizzie, so that she should have a thorough rest. He would come and sleep in the empty cottage, and the laundress would look after him, and he would try to run down if he could, though he was very busy. She was afraid it was a very expensive plan, but it would be such a delicious change; and then, to see the ocean! If only Flora were with her for her first gaze at this wonder, unseen by either! The McCalls were so very, very kind; she felt as if she had known them a great while; and they had even persuaded her to come in once or twice to tea, — no company, of course, only one or two of their relations who were staying with them. Her letters from the Shoals were shorter still, but cheerful; the place was charming, the McCalls all goodness, the children in splendid condition, and she herself better and stronger than she had been since she was a girl. Arthur could not manage to come, which was a disappointment, but he would be surprised to see how well they all were when they came back.

CHAPTER XIII.

ON the morning of the 8th of September, Arthur was busy in his private office, when his boy brought in a card, —

> MR. HAMLIN B. McCALL,
>
> 2000 MAIN STREET,
>
> KANSAS CITY, MO.
>
> Railway Supplies.

"Tell the gentleman I will see him in a quarter of an hour, or if he cannot wait now, at half-past eleven," he said without raising his eyes, and hardly looking at the card. The gentleman preferred to wait, and entered punctually at the close of the stipulated quarter, — a big, ruddy-faced man, middle-aged, but still alert in his bearing, with gray mutton-chop whiskers; more like the popular conception of an Englishman than a

Western man. He was well dressed, though with some little over-display of watch chain, rings, and studs. He began in a loud, cheerful, deep chest voice: —

"Very glad to make your acquaintance, Mr. Butler."

Arthur bowed, and offered him a seat.

"I suppose you have seen by my card where I live, and what my business is," went on his visitor; "I bank with the Merchants' Bank here, and they and my other Boston correspondents, Messrs. Fisk and Waterman, can tell you it's a good one."

"I have no doubt of it."

"I have two blocks of buildings on the best part of Main Street, without encumbrance, and a good lot of land out of town on Western Avenue,— that's our most fashionable residence street,— and sure to rise in value. I am ready to build out there any time a first-class house."

"You are to be congratulated."

"I ain't sure of that yet," said Mr. McCall, laughing and looking conscious; "I'm coming to that point by and by. But now as to my personal character; Reverend Dr. Wilkinson, my pastor, of the First Baptist Church in Kansas City — he's well known at the Baptist Seminary in Newton, where he graduated — can answer for that. I should be glad to have any one write to him, without introduction from me, if they wanted to be sure on that point; I know well enough what he'd say."

Arthur could only bow, wondering what business all this preface portended, but suspecting from the extreme anxiety of his visitor to present his claims to the best advantage that it was not likely to turn out very advantageous to himself.

"My brother, Anson J. McCall, of McCall, Sims, & Stodder — you know them, I suppose — lives out at Newton Centre; he would be very glad to see you any time, and his pastor, Reverend Mr. Close, will let me refer to him with pleasure."

"I dare say it will not be necessary."

"Well, I want to be all fair and square and above board. Living so far off I feel more anxious about it than I should if I were right close by, where I knew everybody, and everybody knew me." He paused with a slight hesitation, and Arthur augured yet more unfavorably of the overtures he was doubtless about to make.

"The fact is," resumed Mr. McCall, drawing his chair a little closer, — "I mean, you might naturally suppose from my age and all that that I'm a married man, but I'm not. I wasn't going to marry till I could keep a wife to suit me. I'm afraid I've waited too long, perhaps, but when I got up a peg in the world, I made up my mind I'd look high. I don't feel inclined to marry in Kansas City, though we have some very fine ladies there, very fine indeed; but I wanted something a little out of the common, and when I come East this summer it was as much for that as anything else. I mean, I thought I'd look about me, and see if I couldn't get something worth waiting for."

He stopped and wiped his face, now a shade ruddier than usual, with his pocket-handkerchief, then proceeded in a jerky style, unlike the confident swing of his commencement.

"I've been staying at my brother's, and then at the Shoals with his family, and I have met a very charming young lady, who is, I believe, your sister-in-law, — Mrs. Orlando Butler." The ice once broken, he went on more glibly; though somewhat constrained by the unresponsiveness of his hearer.

"I've never had much time to cultivate ladies' society, but I ain't sorry for it, if I can only get her to think of me. I never saw any one to equal her — never! I tell you, I'd be proud to take her West! If she won't be admired in Kan' City, I don't know 'em there, that's all."

"My sister-in-law only returned day before yesterday, and I have seen her but once. She did not speak of this to me, but —"

"Bless you! she don't know it! I've said nothing to her about it at all. I wouldn't have felt bound to speak to any one but the lady herself in most cases, but this seemed a little peculiar. Living so far off I wanted to be ahead of her friends, in case they had any objections to make. You seem the only one she's got, and I know she thinks the world of you," looking with some curiosity, faintly tinged with jealousy, at his self-possessed auditor. "She's told me all about your supporting her and the children. It's very good of you, I'm sure, — very good; but you must be wanting to marry yourself by this time," throwing a quick glance at Arthur, "and 't ain't always agreeable in that case to have a whole family upon your hands, and an old mother into the bargain, I believe."

"My sister and her children have never been felt by me to be a burden."

"No offence, no offence, I 'm sure. She's saying all the time how generous you are; and you seem," looking round the room, "to be doing pretty well; but it comes more natural to a woman to be supported by a husband than a brother-in-law, if he 's ever so willing; and even if you were able to marry, and still keep 'em all, why, your wife might n't like it. Now, I 'm willing and able to take the whole family. The children are nice little things, and mighty pretty. The little girl will be a rip-staver, I can tell you, when she grows up. I 'll settle a good bit of my real estate on her, with reversion to them, and if I go on as I hope to, I 'll push the boy ahead, and fit out the girl in style. I always liked children, and at my time of life I don't mind beginning with a pair, — 't ain't like a young man. And she says she 's got a sister, teaching school somewhere in New York State; she can have her to live with her too, and I 'll clothe her well. If she 's anything like Ida — Mrs. Butler — she says she 's handsomer, but that I don't credit — she won't be on my hands long in Kan' City; go off there like hot cakes."

"Mrs. Butler will appreciate your generosity; but I do not think that she has any idea of marrying again."

"How should she?" asked his interlocutor, triumphantly, "when she hasn't been asked? She ain't one to think of a man first. She's a thorough-bred lady, through and through. Perhaps you may think her too good for me, so young as she is, and such a beauty, but she might go further and fare worse. I'll bring 'em East every few years, and first chance I get I'll take 'em all to Europe."

"My sister must decide for herself in such a matter. But you must remember that she has been a widow a very short time, and became one under particularly distressing circumstances, and it will, I fear, be a shock to her feelings to have such a proposal made so soon."

"Why, your brother's been dead a whole year, hasn't he? Lord bless you! I haven't the least doubt that he was an excellent man, but you can't expect her not to marry again, at her time of life! I don't want to hurt her feelings, or to hurry her out of reason; I won't expect her to give me an answer just yet; but I've got to go back to Kansas City in a fortnight or three weeks, and I can't go without I speak to her first, and put the idea into her head at any rate. I can't be back for four weeks, and I dare n't let it go till then; some one else will be sure to come along!"

"Hardly — she lives so very quietly."

"Well, here am I, you see," said the Kansas Citizen, throwing his portly figure back in his chair, "and there 'll be sure to be some one else. It's only fair I should have the first chance. She thinks no end of you, and your advice will go a great way with her. I don't think it'll be fair for you to set her against me, when I've been so open with you from the start."

"I should never dream of advising my sister in such a case, unless there were some very serious reason for it. I do not suppose that there is anything to be known which should prevent her marrying you if she liked you. I will see your brother — I have met him once or twice, and know him well by reputation. He and Mrs. McCall have been very kind to Mrs. Butler."

"Of course they have — they couldn't help it; and Lucy, my sister, she says to me just as soon as I come on East this time: 'Hamlin, if I haven't got just the wife for you I'm mistaken!' Lucy's a right good woman! She longs to have me married, which is real kind-hearted of her, for her children would come in otherwise for my little pile; but they'll have plenty. I can tell you, Lucy'll be pleased! She and all of 'em never knew any one they liked as quick as they did Mrs. Butler. Lucy says she never saw anything so lovely as she looked coming to church in her black, with those two little children, and looking a child herself! You'll think I'm a fool, but wait till you're in love yourself," with another scrutinizing glance at Arthur, who stood it with perfect unconcern. "I suppose you've always thought of her as though she were a sister of your own, and if she were, you might not get a really better chance for her."

"I am sure your attachment is a generous one, and it is due to you that she should know it. As far as I am concerned, you have my full consent; only, I must tell you plainly that I don't think you have the slightest chance."

"That's very proper; that's all I expect you to say," said Mr. McCall. "Lord bless you! I don't expect her to jump at me. Just let me make a beginning;" and he rose and departed, well satisfied.

Arthur made a few inquiries, which seemed amply to confirm everything his visitor had stated about himself, but did not think it necessary to look very deeply into the matter, not expecting to have any further trouble with it; otherwise, he could not have dismissed it so quietly. He had grown to regard the prospect of starting in life with a ready-made family with nearly as much equanimity as Mr. McCall, and Ida was dear to him now for her own sake, as well as her sister's.

He had given up his luxurious quarters in town, and kept a modest *pied-à-terre* there, as well as one in Newton that he might be able to look in upon Ida at any time. He was not surprised when he called that evening to find her in a state of tearful agitation, and helped her to confess what she seemed unable to tell by saying, "I suppose Mr. McCall has been here."

"Yes," said Ida, blushing through her tears, "I am so sorry!"

"So am I. He applied to me beforehand, and I would rather you had been spared this; but I could not refuse my consent to his speaking to you. I had no right to do so. But I told him that I did not think he had the slightest chance."

"No; but I am so sorry for him."

"He seems a very worthy man."

"Yes — oh, yes; he was so very kind to me, and to the children, too, at the Isles of Shoals. He spoke so feelingly of them, and said he would be a father to them."

"Fortunately, my dear Ida, you are not obliged to marry for your children's sake."

"No — oh, no; you are so generous, so very kind. Mr. McCall spoke most highly of you; but he says it would be only natural if you should want to marry yourself some time, and then — "

"He had no business to say any such thing. I hope you told him that I knew he would not please your taste; but it would have been of no use to tell him so, or I would not have let him come."

"I am sure he meant no harm. He spoke of you with great admiration, and said there were very few young men who would have behaved like you. I felt ashamed to think how I had taken it all as a matter of course. I felt as if I had never thanked you as I should."

"Vulgar brute!" muttered Arthur, between his teeth.

"Oh, he did not say it in that way; it was all most kind. It was my fault if too much was said, for I really did not know how to answer him as I ought; I was so surprised, so frightened. I never dreamed at the Isles of Shoals that he was thinking of such a thing. I thought it was only his kindness, and that he was so fond of children. He admired Landy and Flossy."

"What did you say to him?" asked Arthur, feeling that the task of conveying a decided rejection to Mr. Hamlin McCall was to be thrown upon his shoulders, and that he should take a savage pleasure in it.

"Oh, I told him I could n't, not possibly, — it is so soon, so very soon; and I could not think of marrying again at any rate. Of course I could never love any one as I had —" Her voice grew stifled. "But he said he should not ask me to; all he wanted was that I should consent to marry him, and let him devote his life to making me happy. I could hardly get him to go, but I said I could not bear to hear any more," said Ida, relieving herself with a fresh burst of tears.

"He was very selfish to give you so much pain for no use. A man has no right to thrust himself upon a woman in that way."

"I do not think he meant to hurt my feelings. He seems really to be very fond of me. He thinks a great deal more highly of me than I deserve."

"Well, my dear, don't trouble yourself about him any more. If he comes again — and I hope he will not — refer him to me. And now let us talk about something else. Have you heard lately from Liverpool?"

"I have heard from Flora; she does not mention having been there since she last wrote; she cannot get to Liverpool often; but if dear mother were ill, she would be sure to have heard."

"What does she say?"

"You can see the letter if you want to," said Ida, rapidly glancing over it, and satisfying herself that there was nothing private in it, — an expression which she had come to use with a good deal of latitude, authorizing her to allow Arthur to read nine tenths of her letters from her sister, though she never mentioned this to Flora. "She would write with less freedom," she thought; "and it is so natural that Arthur should want to hear all about his mother, and his old home; and mother does not write often now, — it is getting to be an effort to her."

"It seems your letters have been rather short lately," said Arthur, who was devouring eight pages in Flora's delicate legible hand-writing, that would have looked old-fashioned if it had not been so peculiar and characteristic. He could not imagine how she could write so much about so little; but he found it very easy to read, though he was conscious of breathing a rarefied atmosphere as he read her long tales about her school-keeping experiences, and the characters of all the children, and how she was afraid of being partial to Emma Widemeyer, who looked a little like Flossy, only not nearly so pretty. "She speaks of your not having answered some of her questions."

"Oh, yes — it is too bad; but there was so much going on at the Shoals. Poor Mrs. McCall! she and all of them were so kind! I am afraid she will feel very sorry about this. I don't suppose the idea ever occurred to her when she asked me to go there."

"Don't you think she will visit you this autumn?"

"It would be very kind in her, but I am sure her feelings must be hurt. Oh, you mean Flora! no, I don't think she will. I have asked her several times, and told her that I knew you wished it, but Flora is very independent. She told me when she came here that she could not live in your house; but I should think she might make a visit, when you are so kind, and I do so long to see her! Mr. McCall spoke so kindly about her! He wanted her to live with me, and said she should be like his own sister!"

Again Ida seemed tearfully inclined, and Arthur thought it best to leave her to sleep off her worries. He could imagine that her refusal had been couched in the mildest terms, and accompanied with many apologies; but he was not prepared for the appearance of the rejected lover the next morning at his office, in the best of spirits.

"Good morning, Mr. Butler! have you seen your sister?"

"Yes, I called on her last evening."

"How is she?"

"I found her rather painfully agitated."

"Yes, she was a good deal overcome, I

think; she's a delicate little thing. But she gave me all the encouragement I could ask for. I have no doubt it will be all right now."

"I must say I received a very different impression. She told me she did not wish to marry you at all, and that it was most painful to her to have the subject brought before her so soon."

"Lord bless you! what else could she say? She'll say it a good many times yet, of course. But I've no fear but what I can bring her round. Why, if she were dead set against marrying again at any price, there would n't have been so much said about it's being too soon, don't you see? It was her saying that so often that made me see I had a good chance, if I pressed it."

"Perhaps you have, if you press it without regard to her wishes."

"Sho! girls don't know what they wish or want; and Ida, though she's been married, is really but a girl, — more innocent than any girl I ever saw. A country minister's wife, married at seventeen, what should she know of the world? But it's all right; if she'd been a regular widow on the look-out for a husband she'd never have caught me. I don't mean to say anything against your brother, you know. She'll never hear a word from me that isn't most respectful to his memory. It's natural you should feel a little sore on the subject, but it shouldn't make you try to prejudice her."

"I shall do no such thing. I shall only interfere if I see that she is annoyed and harassed by useless persistency on your part."

"Well, we may differ as to how useful it is. I hope I know how to pay my addresses to a lady without making myself disagreeable. She shan't be hurried; I'll give her till I get back from Kan' City to decide. All I ask is that you shouldn't use your influence against me while I'm gone. I know she feels bound to you by affection and gratitude, and all that, — though as to the latter, why, if it comes to that, I'll pay back every cent she's ever cost you."

"If you continue to talk in this way I shall be obliged to ask you to leave my room."

"That's set your back up, has it? No offence. A self-made man like me isn't up to all your fine notions."

"No man can be more self-made than I."

"Well — well — I meant no harm; I'll be proud to owe you something, for I respect your conduct; but you're not her legal guardian, — she's of age; she must take her own way in the matter."

"I do not call it letting a woman take her own way to torment her into marrying you whether she wants to or not."

"I'm only coaxing her for her good, and because I know that I can make her happy — happier than she ever dreamed of before. Wait till you're in love yourself, and then we'll see what you'll stick at."

Arthur, conscience-stricken by a sudden rush of memory which made him see himself caricatured, as it were, before his own eyes, was silent, and his visitor rose, triumphant at having made a good hit, and held out his hand with invincible good-humor. "You mustn't blame me for doing the best I can for myself."

"Good-by, and don't blame me if you don't succeed," said Arthur, taking the proffered hand; for he felt it would be foolish and undignified to pick a quarrel with this man, repugnant as was his presence to him, and doubly repugnant the idea of Ida as his wife. Dear little Ida! he was sincerely fond of her, and, he hoped, unselfishly so. It was the jarring sense of impropriety in this business that hurt him, and his jealousy, if he had any, was for his brother's sake and her own.

He could not trust himself to go near her for a day or two. When he did go, just before tea, he found her little parlor fragrant and brilliant with costly flowers, and herself looking prettier than ever. He thought her dressed with unwonted care, though she had not added to or taken from her usual attire by a single thread; but there was something in the dainty way in which her deep mourning dress was put on beyond her usual matter-of-course neatness; and never did head-dress, surely, sit so exquisitely as that little tulle cap did over her golden locks — just as much less abundant than her sister's as suited her slighter, smaller frame — without some study on the wearer's part of its fitness to the face below. She received her brother-in-law with all cordiality, but shyly, something as she had done when she first came to Newton, before constant intercourse had put them on the easy footing of family life; and looking apologetically at the flowers, murmured that she was very much surprised when they came. The children, who had had their tea before their daily governess had left, now appeared, loaded with new toys, and with an air of expectation which culminated when Mr. McCall appeared. He was very carefully arrayed, and though somewhat taken aback at the sight of Arthur in evening dress, hastened to regain his command of the situation by bringing forward the large basket which he carried, with, "Here, children, here are some peaches for you; I remember your mamma does not approve of candy."

"It is so bad for their teeth," said Ida.

"It would be a shame to spoil such pretty teeth as Flossy's," said Mr. McCall, paring a peach for that young lady, who took it in the daintiest way; for even greediness with her had a grace. "She looks just like you," went on the lover, admiringly.

"She looks much more like her Aunt Flora, after whom she is named; don't you think so?" said Ida, appealing to Arthur, who could not see it. He was fond of Flossy, who was a winning little witch, but surely at her age Flora had been as unique as she was now.

It was not pleasant to him to make a third

in the party, after the children had gone to bed, though Mr. McCall directed most of his conversation to him. Ida said very little, but bent over her work with her delicate blush-rose tint a little brighter than usual, answering very sweetly when spoken to, but seeming well-pleased to listen to a discourse on politics — the tariff — the fall elections — anything that could give them a safe meeting-ground. It could not be denied that Mr. McCall spoke with good sense and moderation on all these topics, nor that his manners, in the presence of the lady of his love, had less of self-assertion than when alone with her brother-in-law. As for her, the wooer had nothing to complain of, whether she intended to accept or reject him at last. She evidently wished Arthur to sit him out, and he on his part made no objection, for he rose and took his leave at a very proper early hour, content with a gracious smile and a few graceful unmeaning words from his hostess.

"I am sorry he will keep coming in this way," she murmured, when he was out of hearing.

"If you do not wish him to, I will let him know that it is unpleasant to you. He is not so ungentlemanly as to persist in the face of your positive commands."

"Oh, no! I could not do that. I could not bear to hurt his feelings when he is so kind; and he goes out to Kansas City so very soon that I think I would not say anything before that. That will put an end to it, most likely." She paused, and as Arthur said nothing she added, timidly, "Don't you think he is a very intelligent man, as well as good-hearted?"

"He seems a good sort of man enough."

"I wish he had not taken this unfortunate — liking for me into his head. I do hate so much to make him unhappy! If Flora had only been here, he would have fancied her instead, and I should have been so glad of that! He would have been just the husband I should have been proud of for her!" Then, a little hurt at Arthur's unresponsiveness, "I do want Flora to have a chance to show something of what is in her! She is, really and truly, a very remarkable girl! Dear Orlando always said so. It seems to me sometimes as if she were wasted where she is; and I, who am not nearly so fit to have things, have such an easy life!"

CHAPTER XIV.

ARTHUR, for the next three weeks, played the part of a passive spectator of Mr. McCall's courtship. The further inquiries which he felt it his duty to make were so satisfactorily answered that he had no excuse for putting forward any objections. Mr. McCall was most anxious to please him, though he did not always know how to do so. In trying to please Ida, Arthur had to allow that he showed more skill. He lavished most of his direct attentions on the children, and treated her with punctilious respect, while sending showers of flowers, fruit, new magazines, and every pleasing trifle which she could not refuse. He took Landy and Flossy to drive with his sister-in-law, a powerful ally, and sometimes, but not always, asked Mrs. Butler to join the party.

He evidently made no more proposals till just before his departure for Kansas City;

but at Arthur's first call after this he found Ida in tears, and when he asked the reason, —

"Mr. McCall was here to-day to say good-by; he said he could not go unless he had — a little — hope; and — and — would you feel very grieved, Arthur dear, if — if — it came to anything?"

"I should have no right, if I thought it for your happiness; if I were sure you knew what you wanted."

"I don't know," said Ida, confusedly plaiting the ribbons of her belt, "I don't know as my happiness is of so much consequence, and he loves me so much! He says he never cared for any woman in real earnest before. It seems cruel to blight his life, because I have had so many sorrows of my own. Of course, you don't suppose that I can ever forget dearest Orlando, or cease to love him and respect his memory. Mr. McCall would never wish for that — he is too good. He is not a bit jealous, and says he will never ask me to give up caring. He only wants me to marry him, and says he doesn't care for anything else; he says he is sure I shall make far too good a wife for him anyhow;" and the faintest of smiles curled her pretty lips as she added, "I wonder what he could see in such a worn-out old thing as I am!"

"Well, my dear Ida, I suppose by this that you gave him some reason to hope."

"Not exactly," said Ida, blushing; "I told him I couldn't decide so quickly; and he said he would wait till he came back for my answer; but — but — when he does come back, I suppose he will be very anxious; and — and —"

"You must not consider him only in this matter."

"But it would be such a good thing for the children; he would be such a father to them! I don't forget — I appreciate fully — all you have done for them, dearest Arthur; it was a great deal more than I had any right to expect, and I don't think I ought to have let you —"

"Ida, if you really feel — I won't say gratitude, for I don't deserve it — but if you feel any affection for me, you will not allow such a consideration to influence you for a moment. I cannot find words strong enough to tell you how utterly you mistake me if you do; but you wrong yourself terribly, if you let it affect your decision in the slightest degree."

"Mr. McCall says you ought to be thinking of getting married yourself."

"If I ever marry, which is certainly not likely at present, I shall have enough to provide for all; and I shall never have a wife who will interfere with my duty to you, or even wish to do so."

"Such girls are not very common. To be sure, I don't expect you to get a wife who is quite good enough for you."

"You are partial, my dear child; but sisters are privileged in that way. As to your own affairs, all I have to say is that I have nothing against Mr. McCall, and I have no right to advise you; but this much I will say, that you must not marry him unless you like him well enough."

Another bright blush on Ida's face almost made words superfluous, but she was not used to keep Arthur waiting for an answer, and she said resignedly, "You surely don't dislike him?"

"I? no; but that is not the point."

"There is a great deal in him to like, don't you think so? All his family are so fond of him; and Lucy, I mean Mrs. Anson McCall, says he is as good through and through as he seems at first sight." She opened a velvet case on her writing-table and took out a photograph. "He had that taken to give me when he left; don't you like it?"

"Very good indeed."

"I don't suppose he is what you would call handsome; but I never cared for that, and I do think he is very fine-looking. He wanted mine so much that I gave him one like that I had taken to send Flora; you don't think that was wrong, do you?"

"Not at all."

"He said he could not live till he came back, without one."

"By the bye, what does your sister say about it?" said Arthur, who had not read Flora's last few letters. He had not found Ida reading one, and he never asked directly for them.

"Flora? oh, she does not know. I never thought of mentioning him at first, and now I don't think it best to tell her till I can tell her something a little more decided. I hope Flora won't mind, and I do hope she'll be willing to live with me, as he wishes. He is sure he shall be very fond of her."

"How is she? What does she say in her last letters?"

"Oh — nothing particular. She is very well. Would there be any harm, do you think, in my answering Mr. McCall's letters, while he is away?"

"No, you could not write a letter which it would do you any harm to have seen."

"Of course I shall write only as a friend," said Ida, satisfied; "he has promised me to say nothing of his proposals till he comes back."

The weeks of Mr. McCall's absence seemed to be regarded by her somewhat in the light of a respite; but Arthur did not expect that another would be asked or granted, and was not surprised when they were over to receive the following note:

NEWTON CENTRE, Oct. 25, 188-.

DEAR MR. BUTLER, — I am proud and delighted to inform you of my engagement to your lovely sister. Ida wishes me to write you the news at once, and excuse her for not doing so herself; but she will be glad to have you call as soon as you can. I am most deeply sensible of the kindness you have shown her and the children, and hope to be regarded in the light of a brother by you. As I expect to see you soon, and tell you all our plans, no more at present from

Your ever grateful and affectionate
HAMLIN B. MCCALL.

Arthur went out to the cottage, and was received by Ida alone, all smiles and tears, but with the former predominating. "Oh, Arthur — you don't mind; you are pleased, are you not?"

"Surely I am, if you are."

"I can't help it, when every one else is so happy. The children, poor little things, are wild with joy. He has just gone out to walk with them, because he thought I would rather see you alone first; he is so considerate. I wanted to tell you that I shall feel just as much your sister as ever, and I hope you will still feel that you are my brother; you have been a better one than many a real one."

"Do not say such things; I don't deserve them."

"I must — and I am sure Mr. McCall agrees with me most fully; and I want to tell you, too, that I shall never forget or cease to love my dear husband. I shall never leave this off," — she looked at her delicate little hand, where an immense solitaire diamond blazed above the slender gold line of her marriage ring, — "but oh, I do think that where he is, he is glad that his wife and children should be so cared for, so cherished. He never had any jealousy either."

"Well, you have chosen, Ida, and I hope for the best. I can only say, God bless you! I shall miss you; but we will not talk of that," he added more cheerfully, as the tears that were gathering in Ida's lovely eyes, threatened to overflow.

"Oh, there he comes with the children, and I had so much more to say to you! I must see you alone again. Stay after he goes away, will you not?"

"If possible, I will," said Arthur, as the door opened, and the children rushed up to him. He was no longer the first object of their attention, but they were delighted to see him, and to inform him that they were going to have a "new papa." Ida, at this, put on a look a little like one of her sister's, to which Mr. McCall responded with, "I hope I'll always be a good father to them; if being as fond of them as one will do it, I shall. If you'll consent to it," to Ida, "I will adopt them legally, and give them my name from the day we're married."

"Thank you," said Ida, "but I would rather my children should keep their father's name;" and she swept onward to the lunch table, now ready in the dining-room for the early dinner, with an accession of dignity, which heightened her lover's admiration, while it amused Arthur, who augured a beneficial training in the matrimonial school for the worthy Kansas Citizen, who was evidently on his best behavior, and painfully anxious to improve.

The elders were all so silent that the lunch-party would have been a quiet one but for the children. Even the demure little middle-aged governess was lamenting the probable loss of a good place, and trying to make up her mind whether or not to accept Mr. McCall's amazing offer to take her with them to Kansas City, since Mrs. Butler and the children were so fond of her, and it would be such an opportunity for her. "It would be a swell thing to have a governess," he informed Ida, in private, "and there's no reason why she shouldn't get a husband out there. She ain't so very old, nor bad-lookin', either."

When she had borne off the children after lunch, Ida said quietly to her betrothed: "I should like to see Arthur alone a few moments before he goes back to town, Mr. McCall. There is a little business I want to speak to him about."

"All right," replied Mr. McCall; "I'll

go round to Anson's for a minute or two. You see, Arthur, I ain't jealous of leaving her with a handsome young man. Now, in return for that pretty speech I expect you to help me persuade her to set the day just as soon as possible."

"I cannot say anything about that till I have told my sister," said Ida.

"Well then, do hurry up and tell her," said the lover, going into the hall for his hat; and returning to say at the door, "and hurry up your talk too, for I'll be back at half-past three with a buggy to give you a ride, little madam!"

"Yes, I will be ready," said Ida, and as he departed, with a lingering look behind, she went on: "It is about Flora that I wanted to speak to you. She does n't know yet, and I don't quite know how to tell her. I don't know how she will feel,—that is, I am afraid she will feel excited, troubled about it."

"Why should she?"

"I don't know; but she will think — she was so fond of Orlando; she will feel very unhappy, I am afraid."

"You must write to her, and explain all your reasons, and she will surely not—"

"Oh, but she can't understand! I don't know how to make her; I have begun several letters, and torn them all up!"

"It is a pity you did not tell her sooner, is it not?"

"Oh, yes, I suppose now it is; but I did not think of — I was not sure of it; and I thought there was no use in worrying her when things were so uncertain."

"But if she knows how good a thing it is for you and that you are happy, surely she will not object."

"You don't know Flora!"

Both were silent for a moment, till Ida, looking timidly up, said, "I cannot tell how to write to her, and I thought —"

"Well!" said Arthur, encouragingly, "what did you think?"

"That perhaps — perhaps — *you* would write," said Ida, looking pleadingly at him. "I am sure you could make her understand a great deal better than I. Tell her I love her so much, just as much as I ever did; and that I shall never forget dear Orlando, but that I did not think I ought to refuse to make some one else happy. And tell her that I am — I mean, that I could be happy myself if I were sure that she was. Tell her that you approve — I mean that you don't mind it *much;* she will think a great deal of that."

"I am afraid I cannot write all this to her," said Arthur; "but if you like, Ida, I will go and tell her myself."

"Will you, — oh, will you? How good, how more than good you are! Then you can see if she minds it very much; if she does," and her tears began to stream again, "I don't know how I am ever to go through with it myself."

"I will tell her all I can; and I can see my mother at the same time, if you wish."

"Oh, thank you; though I know dear mother will not object. She will be glad we are so well taken care of. Tell her that Mr. McCall is a member of a Baptist church. I hope she will not mind my going with him most of the time; he does n't expect me to join it. I told him I could never leave my own." She stopped in her eager flow of talk, and then with a sudden access of shyness: "Flora is going to spend next Sunday at mother's. If you could — "

"Yes, I can go then very well."

"I know Flora will think it is so soon; but then she has n't been here and does n't know. Mr. McCall was so hasty; but he says he had to speak, he could n't help it. But tell her I cannot think of marrying yet, unless she thinks it is proper."

"I suppose Mr. McCall is in a hurry to have the time set?"

"Oh, yes; he says he can only stay here six weeks now, and must run back to Kansas City in the midst of it at any rate. He wants me to go back with him before Christmas; he must be there after that, but I told him I never, never could unless you thought it right; and I want Flora satisfied too, I can't bear that she should think — Oh, there he is! I must hurry and get my hat. Do, Arthur, wait till I come down."

She tripped off, appearing again in a few moments, younger and prettier even than when she went upstairs, so much did every change in her dress tell; and now she had divested her hat of its crape, and advanced to the startling novelty of a violet kerchief round her throat. Arthur walked out to the gate with her and helped her in, and as he carefully tucked in the carriage rug over her dress, she bent forward with a smile, and "Give my very best love to dearest Flora!" and then whirled away, behind a fast trotting horse, while Arthur stood looking after them. "Poor Orlando!" he thought; and then he remembered how presumptuous he had thought his brother in appropriating Ida at seventeen. Why should he not take this common-sense view of the question now?

The betrothed pair, meanwhile, were driving through the shady Newton roads, now radiant in their autumn colors, and Mr. McCall had begun with, "How perfectly beautiful you look to day!" He was in the habit of making such remarks, and Ida, though a little ashamed of herself, could not but own that she did not dislike them. Both Ida and Flora knew of their beauty, as they knew their height and weight, or any other physical trait; but they had too little of the quality of self-absorption to let the fact linger in their minds, whose outlook on the world was all extrospective, to coin a word. Still, no woman but enjoys a man's sincere admiration of her looks. Ida's first brief courtship had been enlivened by few such passages, Orlando's love having been of the kind that does not clothe itself in compliment, and her wedding a hurried, unadorned piece of business. She had never learned coquetry, and now answered in a matter of fact way: "It must be because I have put on a violet scarf for the first time."

"Nonsense! and yet, now I look at it, it is mighty becoming. I remember, the first time I saw you, I thought there was never anything so stunning as you were in your mourning, but now I sort of long to see you in colors. You must have no end of gowns, so I can decide which becomes you best; and speaking of clothes, Ida, you can draw on me to any extent, at any time — you know that."

"Thank you," said Ida; "I prefer that you should not give me my clothes at present. Arthur has never grudged me anything suitable yet, and it is not likely that he will do so now."

"Well done, little madam! it is worth making a blunder to set you up a bit. Let Arthur pay your bills, then; it will show him what he's got before him when he marries. Was that what you were talking so long about?"

"No; there is no hurry about that, yet. I was telling Arthur how much I hated writing to Flora, and I said I wished he would; and he — was n't he kind? — offered to go himself and tell her."

"Whew—w—w!" whistled Mr. McCall; "he knows what he 's about, does n't he? Making up to your sister, that 's plain."

Ida's blue eyes grew round with a stare of unaffected surprise. "What! Flora!" she exclaimed. "Oh, no, I don't believe Arthur ever had any thoughts of her. He has seen so much of the world. Flora and I were only little country girls to him. He will want to marry some Boston young lady, with family and position, and very brilliant and cultivated."

"Well, then, he 'd be a fool, that 's all that I can say, and a snob into the bargain; and I don't think he 's that, though he has a pretty good conceit of himself. I thought at first it was you he had in his mind, he was so confounded stiff when I began on the subject with him; and I was jealous, I can tell you. But I 'd be very glad to have your sister marry him, though I did mean to fit her out in style myself. You 'll see if I 'm not right," as Ida shook her head, smilingly unconvinced.

CHAPTER XV.

THE Friday night train for Syracuse was detained on the road, and it was broad daylight before Arthur traversed the scene of his terrible search little more than a year ago, now settled down into commonplace oblivion, without a trace of the agony that had passed there. Where was there a trace? A little still lingered in Ida's black attire, spite of violet ribbons; and the tightening of his throat, as he passed the indelibly imprinted scene, told him, and he was not sorry, that he should carry one as long as he lived.

He did not reach his mother's house till the middle of the afternoon, — to find it locked and barred. The place looked unlike any of his recollections of it, bearing tokens of the skill with which Mrs. Rand, an efficient, bustling dame, administered Mrs. Butler's allowance. The house was neat, and the garden trim. Some one must soon come home, and he sat down on the well-known bench on the kitchen-door porch, with the autumn wind blowing the red falling leaves of the Virginia creeper about him. There were too many memories rising here, too, to make the hour of waiting a cheerful one. Every now and then the scurrying leaves, as they pattered along the garden path, startled him like a coming tread; but gradually, as thoughts grew deeper, he ceased to notice them, till, when they rustled with the light but measured sound that responds to a real footfall, and Flora appeared coming alone around the corner of the house, he was almost as much surprised as she was. Their eyes met for a moment in an eager look of glad recognition, too brief, too costly for the price that must be paid down for it upon the spot; for Flora in another instant grew deadly pale, and gasped out, "Ida! you have come to tell me that something has happened to Ida!"

"Ida is well, — well and happy. I swear she was when I left her, and that was only day before yesterday. Do believe me; you must believe me."

"The children, — is anything the matter with the children?"

"No, nothing — nothing;" and as she

sank down on the bench from which he had just risen, her heart beating so that he could hear it, "What have I done, — how can I have looked to give you such a terrible fright?"

"I am sorry to be so foolish, but something made me think of — that last time you came; and I don't know why, I could not help feeling that you had something to tell me."

"Cannot I tell you anything you would like to hear, then?" he asked; but he was bitterly ashamed of himself as he watched her trembling subside, and a delicate flush rise on her cheek, just enough to tempt him to go on; he could not while his untold secret lay heavy on his heart, and it was mean, meaner than he could stoop to be, to play on her hopes and fears to win assurance for himself. She tried with a still shaking hand to put the key she carried into the keyhole, but failed, and he took it from her, and opening the door, followed her into the now darkening house, and through the passage into the parlor, and watched her, while with steadier movement she struck a match, and lighted the lamp. She turned to look at him afresh in the growing glow.

"There is something — I am sure there is something," she said, again apprehensive. "Do tell me, and I shall not be so silly. Surely, surely, nothing can have happened to you?" and she regarded him with fixed anxious attention, as if, sound and strong as he stood before her, he might be hiding the loss of an eye, or a limb.

"It is I who am silly, perhaps," he said, "to make such a mystery of what, after all, is a very natural, harmless piece of news; but Ida, somehow, felt some hesitation in telling you, and asked me; and I thought I would rather see you than write." ("Why the devil can't I get it out?" he thought, as he looked at her widening eyes and parted lips, of solemn expectation more than fear, like a child listening to a thunder peal.) "You must remember," he went on, "that your sister is still young, and has a great deal of her life before her; and how shut up she has always been. She has regained so much of her health and strength — you would be surprised to see how well she looks now. I ought not to have been astonished, though I confess I was, but it is the most natural thing in the world that she should want to marry again "

"She cannot! I am sure she would never dream of such a thing!"

"She would not, of course, unless her hand had been earnestly asked for by a man whom she has every reason to believe sincerely attached to her, and deserving of a return." Then, as she looked at him with her incredulity merging into dawning horror: "I am only telling you the truth. God knows it is hard enough for me, if it makes you unhappy."

"How could she? Oh, how could she?" moaned the girl, twisting her hands together, and rocking back and forth in tearless agony.

"Don't — pray, don't feel it so terribly. Dearest Flora, don't — for my sake — I cannot bear it."

"Forgive me," said Flora, trying to stop the restless motion of her hands, "you can't help it. You are very kind; but I could not believe you at first. I have heard of women doing such things, but I never believed one really could; and I never thought that one would be Ida. Oh, Ida! Ida!" she repeated in a less constrained voice; and as a heavy burst of tears made its way, she seemed somewhat relieved, for her nervous motion ceased, and she sat, her face buried in her hands, quite still, except for the long-drawn sobs that shook her when they came. He sat by her, his own heart swelling, and feeling as if he would gladly tear it out if it would do her any good. He longed to take her in his arms and comfort her, but he could not even touch her. Suddenly she raised her head. "Perhaps when she thinks it over, she will see how wrong it is, and give it up."

"I am afraid it is too late; her word is given, and everything will soon be arranged."

"And to think of Orlando! — Orlando, of all men! to be forgotten, not cared for — how could she, how could any one?"

"You should not think so hardly of her. She has not forgotten Orlando. She told me she should never cease to remember him and love him."

"Love him! How can she love him? A woman cannot have two husbands!"

"You told me once how Orlando loved her; do you think he would have wanted to have her unhappy all her life about him?"

"She need not have been unhappy; it is not long to wait; and then, there were the children. Oh, those children! How can she marry another man, who is not their father?"

"Indeed, I think the children will be very well and kindly cared for. I could not have consented if I had not felt sure of that."

"Did she ask you about it?"

"Yes, she did; but I saw that I could not prevent it without using more opposition than I felt to be right. She is of age, and I have no authority over her. She must decide such an important matter for herself, when she once knows all the reasons for and against it; and I had no real reason to give against it. Nobody holds second marriage to be a crime. You must consider, as I said, that there is nothing unnatural in any man's loving Ida, and nothing wrong in her returning it."

"If you were married," burst out Flora, with one of those rare lightning flashes from her eyes that seemed to dry up her tears in a moment; "would you like to think of your wife doing such a thing?"

"No, by God!" he exclaimed instinctively, her beautiful face, dazzling in its pallor, forcing the words from his mouth; "it would make me turn in my grave to think of it!" Then, his excitement urging him on: "But you would never do it."

"No," said Flora, "I never could." She spoke seriously, with as little thought of any personal application of her words as if he and she were already disembodied spirits; "but I should never have thought that Ida could. It seems as if anything might happen now." She was silent a moment, her hands moving restlessly again, like one burning with fever. "If I had only been with her she never, never would, I know! I could not go — how could I?"

"You must not mind that so much. Suppose you had been with her, this particular thing might not have happened; but she would have been capable of it, all the same. It's the being able to do a thing, not so much the doing it, that makes character; we have not much to be thankful for if lack of opportunity be all."

Flora looked up doubtfully, as if inclined to question this; but the sight of tears in Arthur's eyes checked her. It was the only thing he could do for her, but he could have done nothing better; and hers flowed again as she said: —

"I should not have thought she could have done it while she had you; she was always writing about you, and all you did for her, and how good you were. She did not seem to miss me as much as I had been afraid she would; but I never dreamed of this. I do not think she did just right to you when you had been so very good to her; and then, to take the children away from you, when you had once had them! You might have felt a little hurt for yourself."

"So I did," said Arthur, frankly, "but it would have been selfish to have let that affect me. If it had not been for my knowing it I might have advised Ida more strongly against this marriage; and yet, I don't think that would have made any difference in the end. You must remember that this has been coming on me gradually, not suddenly, as it has on you. I do think that Ida ought to have given you some hint, at least, before she made up her mind, and saved you the shock."

"No — it does not matter. I should have tried to do something, then, and very likely done something wrong, and it might have been of no use, after all. I don't seem to understand how Ida feels about it, or what she thinks. She is like a stranger, and not Ida."

"I do not in the least suppose that she

would have married again, certainly not so soon, if Mr. McCall had not been so very determined to have her."

"Is that his name?" asked Flora, with a shudder, as if some noxious animal were in question.

"Yes, and he is a very worthy, kind-hearted man. He can give your sister many more advantages than I can. It was partly the consciousness of this that kept me from showing any wounded feelings I might have — for I was hurt, I confess," he added, smiling.

The confession seemed to please her, and she said with gratitude in her look: "I am glad you minded it too. I don't mean to be selfish, and I want — I do want to have Ida happy; but I do not feel as if this could ever be right. I hope," she went on anxiously, "that she said — that she knows how much she owes to you."

"Yes, indeed, they have both said all that was proper for them to say, and more than I deserved or expected, — more than I wanted; but I am sure he is a well-meaning man, if he does not always suit me in everything. I am sure, very sure, he will be good to her and the children; and as to you, he is most anxious to be a friend to you. He wants you to come and live with them, and be like his own sister, and I have no doubt he means it."

"I cannot do that."

"Ida wishes it so much. I think she will be very unhappy if you do not come. I do believe she loves you better than anything else in the world."

"I cannot do it."

"She sent you more love than I can find time to give you, I fear; and now she will write herself directly, as soon as she knows you have heard;" and as she made no reply: "It pains me more than I can say to give you pain, but it would not be right not to tell you that she and Mr. McCall both want you to give up your school immediately and come to them. He will gladly pay any sum required to supply your place till the end of the term, and Ida says she cannot be married unless you are at the wedding, and that she will not fix the time until she hears when you can come."

"I cannot come."

"Ida will be very much grieved."

"Oh!" said Flora, with a long sigh of utter exhaustion, "I cannot help it! I have tried and tried to do things, but there was always some use in them; now there is no use in anything. Ida does not really need me now. Can't you — won't you tell her how it is, and that I do love her, and wish them both well and happy, but — I cannot live with them; I cannot live under his roof and eat his bread."

"Yes, I will make that all right; don't trouble yourself about it any more," he said, alarmed at her agitated breath, and the throbbing flush that came and went on her temples.

"And do you think that I am doing wrong?"

"No, indeed, I do not." Words of praise — of love — rose to his lips; but he recognized the fact that to one sick at heart, sugar-plums were loathsome. "I understand perfectly how you feel, and I know just what you want me to say to Ida; you may set your mind at rest about that. There is my mother at the gate with Mrs. Rand;" and as she looked nervous and frightened: "You had better go upstairs and leave me to see her; go to bed, and don't come down again to-night. Your head aches terribly, I am sure."

"Yes," said Flora, putting her hand to her head, mechanically, "but that is no matter."

"Do go," he repeated, and she rose, instinctively obedient, and with a languid "Thank you" dragged herself out of the room, and up the stairs, before the elder women bustled in from the sewing society, laden with work-bags and cap-boxes.

CHAPTER XVI.

MRS. BUTLER had no reason now to dread her son's appearance, but her greeting was confused, perhaps from habit, and he thought, or fancied, she was more slow in recovering her composure than formerly. She heard his news with some little surprise, but with satisfaction.

"It is wonderful," she said with fervor, "to think how the Lord provides for the widow and orphan! Poor, dear Orlando! How thankful would he have been could he have been spared to know of this! Truly, we may say with the sweet singer of Israel, 'I have never seen the righteous forsaken, or his seed lacking bread.' Where is Flora; has she not come yet? You say he wants her to live with them?"

"Yes, he offers to treat her like a sister of his own."

"Well," said Mrs. Butler, wiping her eyes, "I shall miss dear Flora, but I would not be so selfish as to object to what is for her good; and as Mr.— what did you say his name was?"

"McCall, — Hamlin McCall."

"You said he was a Christian, did you not?"

"I don't remember; but he is a member of a Baptist church, if that makes him one."

"I have known a great many good Baptists," said Mrs. Butler.

"Yes," said Mrs. Rand, "there's good and bad in them, as there is in every denomination, and some must be mighty good to make up for the others."

Mrs. Butler seemed to shrink from some personal application in these words, and said meekly, "Mr. McCall will not expect Ida and Flora to become Baptists, will he?"

"No; Ida is willing to attend his church with him, but he will not expect her to join it."

"The girls both joined their father's church when they were very young, and I don't think they would like to give it up. I have heard Mr. Shepherd was rather lax; Dr. Todd, who knew about him, said he even doubted the eternal punishment of the heathen; many Congregational clergymen in New England do, I hear. But Orlando always said a better Christian than Miss Esther could not be, and I am sure Flora is one. I am confident that prosperity will not spoil her."

"Probably not; as she does not intend to accept Mr. McCall's offer."

"Why not?" asked Mrs. Butler, amazed.

"She does not like the idea of Ida's marrying again."

"Dear me! dear me! that is very singular; surely there is nothing wrong about it. Saint Paul expressly says to Timothy, 'I will that the younger women marry;' and Dr. Todd says that the context shows he included widows."

"Well," said Mrs. Rand, "you and I ain't followed Gospel teachin', then. To be sure, I was gettin' on when I lost Mr. Rand; but you was young enough, Mrs. Butler."

"I had my chances," said Mrs. Butler, bridling a little, "and some good ones; but none that I could conscientiously accept. Mr. Montandon, the wealthy butcher from Utica, wanted to marry me, and was most generous in his offers; but he was a Universalist, and I wouldn't have anything to do with him unless he became a Christian.

Then Deacon Hiland, father to the present deacon, — he was a very pious man, but he did n't want to be troubled with the boys, and said if I married him they must all be bound out as soon as they were seven, and I could n't bear to think of that. Did you say Flora did n't like it?" she asked after looking for her knitting-bag, which hung on her arm the while.

"Not at all."

"That's very strange. I shall talk to her about it. She ought not to object if I don't, and I'm sure no one loved poor Orlando more than I did. But I know if he were here that he would be the first one to rejoice in it. He was so very unselfish. Where is she?"

"She has gone to bed, and I think she had better not be disturbed."

"No," said Mrs. Rand; "let her sleep it off; and you, Mrs. Butler, you'd better be goin' to bed yourself. She always goes to bed early society evenings, she gets so tired," she explained, and Mrs. Butler, who was evidently accustomed to obey her companion, after a little more fussing, departed.

"I guess the old lady's mind is beginnin' to fail," said Mrs. Rand, cheerfully, after she had gone. "She gets very confused now whenever she's tired."

"She cannot be old enough for that!" said Arthur, starting.

"She *is* young to break up," said Mrs. Rand, "but she's worked hard in her day, and I guess she wa'n't never very strong." Mrs. Rand was fond of Mrs. Butler, and appreciated her comfortable position with her, but it was her wont to hail all happenings with a sort of desperate cheerfulness. She went on: "I wish Jonah would let her alone; he keeps writing for money all the time."

"Does she send it?"

"Gracious, no! I don't let her have any. She got a letter from him this morning, and that kinder put her out. I wrote and told him to ask you himself. I guess he won't do that yet awhile. It's them Hewsons that put him up to it; and it makes her feel real bad that they should act so when they're church members. I was real provoked that it should happen to-day when Florer was comin', because she's been lookin' forward to that. Florer pets her up, you see, and does a lot of things for her that I can't get time for, and I don't know as I'd have the patience to fiddle with them, neither," concluded Mrs. Rand, stopping to take breath.

"I am afraid Miss Shepherd will not be able to do anything to-morrow. Please do not let her be disturbed."

"Oh, she'll get over it! Girls have their fancies, and Florer has no end of 'em, though she's the nicest girl I ever seen by a long chalk. She'll be all right to-morrow."

Arthur did not feel so sure of that; and when he had drunk a cup of Mrs. Rand's tea, with accompaniments more appetizing than he was used to there, he left the house to its early darkness, and wandered disconsolately off to believe himself by unburdening as many of his cares as he could bring himself to, to Dr. Griscom, — the process being easier for his conviction that his confidant knew a great deal more than he was told.

The doctor thought Mrs. Butler far from strong, but did not know why with care she might not live for many years; "and you are doing all you can for her," he wound up.

"Yes — I am doing all I can for her, now."

"You always did that."

Arthur said nothing, and the doctor looked for something further to follow to account for his visitor's evident low spirits, and listened with a more lively interest to the second part of his tale.

"So! Ida's going to be married again!" he commented. "Well — well! I shouldn't have thought she'd have wanted to do it quite so soon. I suppose you didn't either?"

"Hardly. I don't know that she wants to now, but Mr. McCall wants to have her, there is no doubt of that."

"Poor child! I don't suppose she ever did know what she wanted; she never had the chance. If she had ever had her own way she might know how to take it now."

"I think she will have some chance of learning."

"Yes? Well, if she isn't happy and he too, it will not be her fault. She is a dear little thing, but hardly strong enough to go through all she has. Poor Orlando! he was a good fellow if ever there was one. They loved each other fondly; and yet if she had died first, — and I've expected it, more than once, — most likely he'd have married again. There's hardly a country minister that hasn't used up more than one wife. Well — well — I've done it myself; but, Lord help us! we haven't learned yet not to expect more of women." The doctor ran on, trying to dissipate some of his own wounded feelings, as well as what he fancied were his companion's; and meeting no response, he stopped and put the question direct: "How does Flora like it?"

"Not at all. Indeed I fear she will make herself ill over it. She has gone to bed now; but if she is not better in the morning I wish you would go and see her."

"Oh, yes, I'll go and see her; but you needn't worry yourself; let her sleep it off, and cry it off. She is but a baby yet; she'll have to live and learn, like the rest of us; she'll know better when she's older."

"I hope not," said Arthur, decidedly.

"Well," said the doctor, with a sudden change of expression, "perhaps she won't, if *you* never teach her!"

Arthur called at his mother's early the next morning, but Flora was not visible. "She says," said Mrs. Rand, "that she's got too bad a headache to get up; but don't be scared, she ain't goin' to be sick. She's real silly! I bet I could get her up by scoldin' her a bit; but somehow I don't make no good hand at scoldin' Florer."

Arthur lingered disconsolately about till

the doctor called, and went upstairs, where he stayed a great deal longer than was sufficient to administer a dose of antipyrine, which he declared was all the medicine his patient needed. But when he came down he brought with him two open notes, one addressed to Ida, the other, as Arthur recognized with a great throb of the heart, his own first letter from Flora. They ran as follows: —

LIVERPOOL, Oct. 29, 188–.

DEAR MR. BUTLER, — I am very sorry that I cannot see you again before you go. Thank you for coming here, and all your kindness. I have written to Ida. Will you please, if it is not too much trouble, read it, and if you do not think it says what is just right, destroy it, and tell Ida I will write as soon as I am able. I do not know just what to say, but I don't want to make her unhappy. Pray, tell her so, and give her my best love. I am very sorry that you are going to have all the care and trouble about this, and that I have made you more instead of helping you any.

Yours very sincerely,
FLORA MARY SHEPHERD.

LIVERPOOL, Oct. 29, 188–.

DEAR IDA, — Please don't mind if I cannot come. I do hope you will be happy, I do indeed; and if my coming would make you any more so, I would try, but I know it would not. I am afraid I am not fit to be at any place where every one ought to be cheerful. I wish I were, for I do love you — you know I do — just as much as ever, and I am sure you do me. You have been away in new places, and among new people, and it is not strange, perhaps, that things look different to you. I suppose last year seems a long time ago to you, but oh! to me it is like yesterday. I cannot help it, though perhaps I ought. Kiss my darling Landy and Flossy for me a thousand times, and tell Mr. McCall I wish him all happiness. I am sure he is a good man, or Mr. Butler would not have been willing you should marry him. God bless you dearest!

From your ever-loving sister,

FLORA.

P. S. Mr. Butler has said all you could have wished him to, in the very kindest way.

FROM ARTHUR TO FLORA.

LIVERPOOL, Oct. 29, 188-.

DEAR MISS SHEPHERD, — Thank you very much for your note, and for letting me see that to your sister, which I shall give her, as I do not see how you could write differently. It is much the best way to be truthful, if it hurts at first. I will see that she fully understands. I am very sorry to leave without seeing you again, but must go to-night, as I have important engagements for Monday. Dr. Griscom has promised not to let you go back to Cold Spring until he thinks you quite able, and to write to me how you are, or I could not go.

    Your devoted

        ARTHUR BUTLER.

 Arthur would have liked to treat his resolution by sending some flowers with this note, but did not feel that he had the right to expose Flora to the comments and inquiries of his mother and Mrs. Rand, and he journeyed back to Boston, reading and re-reading her two little notes, till the one to Ida began to show too visible signs of wear. He had them by heart, but it was refreshing to touch the paper her hands had held. These letters were the only gifts that had ever passed between them, and as he folded hers away in an inner compartment of his note-case, never to leave him till he had another, he smiled rather sadly at his own sentimentality, and then wondered where Flora would keep hers.

 He found Ida lovely, bright, and beaming after four days of Mr. McCall's society without the *memento mori* of his own presence. It seemed cruel to plunge her at once into successive depths of surprise, disappointment, and despair. For the next six weeks his own worry and harass were distracting. Ida wished her wedding to be indefinitely postponed, and showed, without losing an iota of her sweetness and gentleness of manner, more strength of will than he had given her credit for. It was he himself who put his to bear down hers, and as might be expected, successfully. He felt that things had now gone too far for such a step to be properly taken, and that her betrothed husband's claims could not be ignored. He was powerfully seconded by Mr. McCall, of whom his opinion was highly raised before the wedding came off. That he should show no jealousy of Arthur, in or out of Ida's presence, though it spoke him thoroughly good at heart, was not surprising; but his holding back himself from all active persuasion, and leaving his cause in the other's hands, evinced diplomatic talent which one would hardly have given him credit for. He gained immensely by it, as Ida's interviews with Arthur were all marked by tears and arguments, and those with him by soothing and consolation. She drew nearer to him through it all, and when at last on a bright frosty morning in early

December, Arthur led her up the aisle of the great empty church to meet the quietest and smallest of wedding parties, she looked, under all her modest shrinking, a sufficiently willing bride to gladden a bridegroom's heart. The sorrow at her sister's absence, which softened her eyes with liquid dew, and sent one or two drops down the blushing roses of her cheeks, was only deep enough to simulate well a maiden's becoming regret at leaving home. She had never looked more beautiful, perhaps because for the first time in her life she was beautifully dressed, — in rich cloth of the palest silvery gray, trimmed with costly gray fur, and a picturesque beaver hat and feathers to match, with delicate rose satin showing in the lining, to match the pale pink roses in her hand, — all, and much more, Arthur's last gifts to his now fondly loved sister, the only one to whom he acknowledged such a tie. He remembered certain dreams of one day giving such things to Flora, — since grown more vague and doubtful; and as he watched the heavy ring slide on to Ida's small hand, where the slender little token of her first marriage had been smothered in gold and gems, he felt as if it marked the snapping as well as the binding of a tie. He had not much time to think before it was over, and Mrs. Hamlin McCall was surrounded by all her enraptured new relations. The newly married pair were to set out from the church door for New York, where the Anson McCalls were to meet them the next week with Miss Meade and the children, who, according to their mother's very decided wish, were not present at the ceremony.

The bridegroom was in no way disturbed that his bride at parting clung to her brother-in-law in a shower of tears. "Come on to New York next week, Arthur," he said heartily, "and visit us at the Fifth Avenue, and we'll have a regular blow-out in honor of this wedding. She'll be all ready to celebrate it by that time, I know; hey, Ida? There, you've got to leave him some time or other; but he shall put you into 'the carriage — he deserves it;" and he himself turned on the step after his wife was in to give Arthur an emphatic shake of the hand, with, "'T will be your turn next, I hope."

Arthur looked after them, conscious of some relief that the thing was fairly over. He was tired out by the strain of it, and not at all disposed to take up the dreary post-festal tasks of paying the bills, closing the cottage, and storing the furniture. He had much to do that usually falls to a woman's share, and he had not even a woman's advice. He did not accept the invitation to New York; but his labors were enlivened by the following letters: —

FROM MRS. BUTLER TO ARTHUR BUTLER.

LIVERPOOL, Dec. 14, 188-.

MY DEAR ARTHUR, — We have been much excited at the arrival of dear Ida and her good husband. They stopped at Syracuse with the darling children, Miss Meade, their worthy governess, and Christine, their French nurse, who seems an excellent person, though a Catholic, — a delightful party. Mr. and Mrs. McCall rode out with the children to see us that very afternoon, and they asked Mrs. Rand and me to spend the very next day at their hotel with them; also Flora, whom they had telegraphed to, and who had come here to meet them; which she could do very well, as it was Friday. I told them I seldom went into such gay scenes, and they must excuse me. But Mr. McCall would not take no for an answer, and Ida came out by herself the next morning in a splendid carriage drawn by two horses, and took us first to the cemetery, where we visited our lot — where dear Orlando's remains and those of his precious babe repose. She seemed much affected, and said she should bring her children the next time they came East; just now she thinks them too young to understand.

Mr. McCall is a noble-looking man, and a true Christian; he paid me the very highest honor and respect, not looking down on my humble cottage, though so wealthy. I hope he will not be more extravagant than a Christian should be. I was almost alarmed at the elegant dresses worn by Ida; she said you gave them to her. I fear you did not remember what snares such things are to the soul.

The children are much grown and improved. I think Miss Meade a very fine lady, though much grieved to find out that she was a Unitarian, — a sect, I believe, much like the Universalists here, and foes to Evangelical truth. I wish you had chosen otherwise, — even an Episcopalian would have been better than one who is not a Christian at all; but she seems a lady of great learning, and was very kind and affable to me.

Dear Ida was full of kind attentions to us all, and rejoiced especially at meeting her beloved sister after so long a separation. She brought Flora and me many lovely gifts from New York, — a beautiful black satin dress piece for me, and a copy of the Holy Scriptures, beautifully illustrated by a talented young Frenchman, named Doré; and an exquisite little cabinet from Japan, — knowing how much I have always been interested in the narratives of the missionaries about that lovely but benighted land. She gave Flora a white silk for a gown, which she said would wash, and a gold brooch, and an elegant box with brushes and combs, and other articles. Oh, and I forgot to tell you, she gave us both her photograph and the children's, and Mr. McCall's. Flora did not wish to take the presents, but Ida felt so unhappy about it that at last she consented. I hope Mr. McCall did not think her ungrateful. She has very peculiar ideas. He, and Ida, too, are very earnest that she shall go and live with them, but she positively refuses. I felt it my duty to urge her not to neglect such advantages, but cannot be sorry to have the dear girl remain so near me, though she will not come here nearly as often as I want her to.

I am very tired, so must defer till another opportunity the description of the day in Syracuse, and the superb dinner at the hotel in a private dining-room. John and Almira, with Laurea, and Dr. Griscom, came afterwards, and stayed to tea. Ida had presents for all of them, and some to send to Jonah and his wife. I am happy and thankful to hear from Jonah that he has joined the Baptist Church, and been immersed, as I told you he intended, and is, I hope, walking a consistent course; but he seems distressed for money. I hope you will find it in your power to help him with a little. The Lord has blessed you with prosperity; oh, forget him not!

and remember that he may be sought and found, even at the eleventh hour!

From your affectionate mother.

FROM IDA TO ARTHUR.

Palmer House, CHICAGO, Dec. 15, 188–.

DEAREST ARTHUR, — We are stopping here for a few days, as Mr. McCall has business, and thought it would be a good chance to show us the city; so I have time to write you about our visit to Syracuse and Liverpool. I could not then, — so much was going on all the time, and so many memories were brought back. I don't know that I should have had the courage to stop there, though I did so long to see dear mother (I shall never call her anything else) and dearest Flora, but Mr. McCall was so kind, and insisted upon it. He has been so invariably good and kind! I wish I were worthier his love and care.

I cannot tell you how I felt when I saw the dear old place again once more. I could do nothing but cry, and Flora too, though she does not seem to feel quite so unhappy as I have feared ever since I first heard from her. Oh, it is such a relief to have seen her! She looks beautiful, but rather tired, I thought. I felt so mean to have her working away at school-teaching, while I am so coddled and petted; but it is not Mr. McCall's fault. He would only be too thankful to have her come and live with us. She will not consent yet, but I have great hopes of persuading her in time. Can't you advise her to? She thinks so much of your judgment.

Mr. McCall thinks her a perfect beauty. I hope she really likes him. She says he seems to be very nice; but one must live with him to know how really, truly good he is. He did not at all wonder that I wanted to visit the sacred spot where my dear ones are laid, and said he thought I had better go without him this time. Sometime we will bring our children together. How beautifully you have had the place kept! And Flora, too, has visited it often, and seen to the flowers. I could not help feeling, as I stood there, that dear Orlando knows all, and is glad with and for me and his children.

I found dear mother looking pretty well; but she seems to get tired and confused much more easily than she used to. Mrs. Rand seems attached to her, and is, I should think, an excellent person to be with her. I hope you will soon go and visit her, for she feels lonely, with her family so scattered. Flora has spent another Sunday with her, which is a great pleasure to them both, and the doctor is very attentive.

Mr. McCall has come in, and wants me to come out for a drive with him on the lake shore. The sleighing is very fine here now, so I must go, though I have a great deal more to say; but I am ever and ever

Your grateful and loving sister,

IDA.

FROM DR. GRISCOM TO ARTHUR BUTLER.

LIVERPOOL, Dec. 15, 188–.

DEAR ARTHUR, — I suppose you have heard that we have had the bridal party here, including children, governess, French maid, and little dog, and I won't say how much baggage, but Mr. McCall appears competent to engineer it all. He made a pleasant impression here; and "little madam," as he calls her, seems well disposed to be happy, in spite of a few natural tears. She looked charmingly pretty, and was as sweet and affectionate to all her old friends as ever. The man must really be excused for falling in love with her.

It was a hard strain on poor Flora, but it did not last long, and she behaved very well, — just as she should. The worthy McCall seemed rather amazed at her appearance. He was very ready to second all Ida's entreaties about her living with them; but he told me privately he did not expect her to accept them. I think he can put two and two together as well as most men.

Your mother enjoyed the meeting very much, but felt fatigued afterwards. She seems weaker than I thought, and shows a lack of recuperative power. I will keep my eye upon her without alarming her, and let you know if she has any decided symptoms. Meanwhile believe me

Yours very truly,

BENJAMIN F. GRISCOM.

FROM JOHN BUTLER TO ARTHUR BUTLER.

CUBITT AND BUTLER, CHINA PARLORS.

SYRACUSE, N. Y., Dec. 29, 188–.

DEAR ARTHUR, — I write to say that mother has had what seems to be a paralytic stroke. The doctor sent for me, and asked me to telegraph you, but I thought it hardly worth the expense, as she has rallied some and is in no danger just yet, and I did n't know as you would care to come on so soon again. She can speak, though not very plain, and she asks to see you, but Almira thinks she don't know what she 's talking about.

Mrs. Rand says she thinks she 's been running down for some time, though she 's been going about to church and everywhere. The doctor says she may live a good while yet, but this was a pretty serious one for the first; so I don't look to see her ever get back to where she was before. Mrs. Rand says she must have some one to help her, but Almira thinks she could get along perfectly well, as mother is very quiet; but I don't suppose Mrs. Rand will stay without some one, or more pay. I don't know how you will feel about it. I am sorry I can't do more at present than I am doing. I paid for all the repairs on that house last year, except putting in water upstairs, which you can't call a repair exactly; and I 've had a great deal to do to my own house this year, besides enlarging the store. Very likely Ida's husband would do something if he was asked. He seems rich, though Almira says it may be all show; but they do dash out, there's no mistake. Ida looked stunning when she was here. I should ask them, at any rate.

There is no other news here, except that the Hewsons are going to California, and Jonah and his wife with them. They are going to join a Bellamy co-operative colony. I don't suppose it will last long, as they've got Jone in it; but as some of them were fools enough to put in money, it may keep up a year or two. Almira sends her love. Please write soon and tell me what to say to Mrs. Rand. With regards of

Your brother,
JOHN BUTLER.

CHAPTER XVII.

ARTHUR spent his New Year's Eve in the night train for misnomered Syracuse, whose shabby station loomed up, in the dim light of the early winter morning, darker than ever against the pure whiteness of the freshly fallen snow-drifts, whiter than the quarried marble of her ancient forerunner. He did not go near his brother, whom he had no wish to meet till all his arrangements were made, but took his way with as little delay as possible to Liverpool and to his mother's house, where Mrs. Rand greeted him with, "Well, Mr. Butler! I didn't think you'd be here so soon! but I'm glad you've come, and that's a fact."

"How is my mother?"

"She ain't much changed since she was first took. Seems as if she felt worse to-day than usual, because Florer's just gone."

"Miss Shepherd has been here, then?"

"Yes," said Mrs. Rand, who looked as if she thought this ceremonious address a waste of breath; "she come as soon as she heard your ma was sick, and stayed here till to-day. She could, you know, because it was vacation-time. I don't know what I 'd done without her; she can make out what Mrs. Butler wants better 'n I can. School don't begin till day after to-morrow, but she would n't stay because she. said you 'd be sure to come. I suppose she thought you 'd want her room; that is, I 'll take it, and give you mine, for hers opened into your ma's. If you 'll set with the old lady a bit, I 'll tidy up — that is, unless you want your breakfast."

"I have had it, thank you. You must not let me incommode you. I can get a lodging out."

"I 'd full rather you 'd stay here, at least till I see what 's going to be done. I 'd as soon not be in the house with her alone, over night."

"You must have some one to help you, certainly; that is, if you wish to stay. My brother wrote that you might perhaps want to leave."

Mrs. Rand gave an inarticulate snort of contempt. "Yes, pretty likely that I 'd be leavin' just as she 's took sick! I 'd thank Almirer not to be sayin' things about me.

No, I'll stay and see Mrs. Butler through, if I'm spared myself. She and I was always good friends. I told 'em I knew you'd do what was proper, and they needn't bother themselves."

"I am much obliged to you. I will stay till something is decided."

"Florer's going to see if she can get Lena Snyder to come and wash to-day; she's a good hand to work, and perhaps she'd stay, if she was asked. She —"

"I thought you said Miss Shepherd had gone back to Cold Spring," Arthur contrived to get in.

"Yes, she's gone; the doctor was a-goin' to drive her, and she said she'd stop at Snyder's on the way. The doctor'll be back at dinner-time, if you want to see him," went on Mrs. Rand, as she led the way upstairs.

Arthur sat with his mother an hour or two, while Mrs. Rand bustled in and out, until Lena Snyder, a short, apple-cheeked German woman, arrived, and tying on her blue-checked apron, set to work in a matter-of-course fashion, and Mrs. Rand came up and released him. It was weary work to sit by Mrs. Butler, who looked pleased to see her son at first, and again whenever she took cognizance of his presence; but she seemed trying with painful effort to keep her mind at a point from which it would perpetually slide, just as she was endeavoring to make her words understood, evidently aware that something was the matter, though uncertain what it was, or whether it was in herself or her hearer.

"They sober down and get quieter when they get used to it," said Mrs. Rand; "she won't be so restless long. Now what is it, — your handkerchief? No? She'll use one word when she means another, till you've gone through everything you can think of, and perhaps tain't any of 'em. Florer could understand her real quick — oh, it's her she wants," as the patient struggled to get out the name, and succeeded. "Well, she can't come now; she's got to go back to school; but she'll be comin' back on Sabbath-day. Now, Mr. Butler, you'd better go down and have your dinner, — it's all ready; and I'll set with her. Most likely she'll go to sleep soon."

"Did Miss Shepherd say she would come back on Sunday?" inquired Arthur, as she followed him to the door.

"No, she did n't; but gracious! your ma don't know what day it is. There ain't no harm in tellin' her things. She'll have forgot it all when Sunday comes."

Arthur was not so sure of that. There was a sense to him of comprehension in the questioning imprisoned soul. He had no appetite for his lonely dinner; but as he walked to the doctor's the fresh keen air set every nerve thrilling with the joy of health and strength. There was a difference in being out under the cloudless blue heaven, upon the shining white earth, which seemed so much wider than when it was green, and being shut in by prison walls that must narrow day by day, and hour by hour. He would do what money could to alleviate his mother's condition; but that seemed like nothing at the moment.

The doctor's house was a good one, one of the best in the place, and boasted of a double parlor with sliding doors; but since the last Mrs. Griscom had died, and the last Miss Griscom had married, this apartment was rarely entered. The doctor inhabited his office on the other side of the hall, in front of the dining-room, where for a brief space after his early dinner he was once in a while to be found, — his only approach to office-hours. He was not there now, and the only person waiting was a young lady, who looked up as the door opened.

"How do you do, Miss Shepherd? I did not expect to find you here."

"No, I have been waiting for the doctor since nine o'clock. I expected him long before now."

"I suppose he is never certain."

"No, but he promised to take me back; he will come home sometime to-day, at any rate."

"A re-assuring prospect!" said Arthur, gravely, seating himself in the doctor's own arm-chair. "Have you had any dinner?" for she looked pale and tired.

"Yes, Mrs. Prince said that it was a pity some of it should not be eaten before it was cold, and that very likely the doctor would get his out somewhere, and come back in a hurry to be off."

"He leads a hard-worked life, does he not?"

"I think he likes it," said Flora. It seemed each time a great effort for her to speak, but she went on: "How did you find Mrs. Butler?"

"Much the same as when you saw her, I suppose; only she misses you a great deal."

Then, as she made no answer: "It was very kind in you to go there."

"I could not help it."

"How was Ida when you last heard from her?"

"Very well; has she not written to you since she went to Kansas City?"

"Yes, once; of course she is very busy. I do not expect her to keep it up."

"There is the doctor," said Flora, with an air of relief.

"How do you do, Arthur? I did not expect to find you here. Well, Flora! tired of waiting? It's too bad. I've been at Van Buren, where one of the Germans chose to keep his *Schutzenfest* last night with an old gun that burst when it went off, and I've been probing him for the pieces. Oh, he'll get over it; he's a tough customer," as Flora grew paler. "They've not been starving you here, have they? Let me have a snack, for I'm hungry, and I'll drive you back directly. Your mother is n't worse, Arthur, is she?"

"No; I only wanted to ask you a few questions about her."

"Come and sit by me for five minutes while I have my dinner; I've no time to lose, — three or four calls to make on my way back."

"You had better let me drive Miss Shepherd to Cold Spring, if she does not object; that will save you time, and of course, be very agreeable for me."

"I think you had better — much better. It will give me time to eat my dinner like a Christian. I'll tell them to harness Fly into the cutter for you; he's rather slow, but you've got the afternoon before you; and Jessie, when she's had her oats, will do well enough for me in the pung. Flora, my dear, you don't object, do you?" with a twinkle in his eye, as he left the room.

Flora resignedly drew on her jacket and buttoned her gloves, and when the cutter came to the door, she let the doctor help her in, and settle the rug carefully round her feet, without a look at Arthur. There was intense delight in being with him, and she was not going to refuse anything he might ask; but she longed, as so many women have longed in vain, to be understood as well as loved. Sometimes she had felt that she was; but she knew she could not expect it now.

"I hope you do not mind my coming with you," he began, when they were well clear of the village.

"No," said Flora, "I am very glad to see you."

"If I had not found you here, I should have come to Cold Spring to see you." Then after a pause, which she did not break: "You have seen the state my mother is in. I cannot tell how long it may last. The doctor says a few years, but not many. She needs some one to care for her, and she has no daughter. There is no one she loves better than she does you. She will know you and want you as long as she wants anything. And then, do you remember what you said to me when you and I last met, — that you could not bear to have Orlando forgotten? You do not forget; you are unhappy because you cannot. I thought perhaps you would be glad to have a chance to do something for him still."

"I should be, very," said Flora, with a great sigh of relief.

"And I thought," he went on, — "forgive me if I am wrong, — but it seemed to me that last time that you were sorry for me, and that you felt that I had a little reason to be hurt on my own account by Ida's marriage. I thought perhaps you would like to do something, you don't know how much, for me; something I could never do for myself."

"Yes, indeed, I should!"

"Will you come and live with her and take care of her? Don't promise till you understand. If you come, you must let me give you all you need; you can't live quite on nothing. Don't be frightened," he said, smiling; "I shall not give you more than I should any one else who was equally competent,— perhaps less, for I don't know any such person; but I shall not let you wear yourself out; that would be foolish, when I have enough to provide you with proper help. If you come, will you let me arrange these things as I think best, and trust me that it is so?"

"Yes," said Flora, very low.

Arthur and Flora were wont in their after life to look back upon the period that now began for them as a happy one, though of such happiness as rarely comes to youth; more like the quiet days of late middle life, when without age's feebleness there is something of age's peace. They never planned what their lives were to be when it was over, sure only that they were to be spent together. They never asked how long it would last, for Mrs. Butler failed so surely, though slowly, that they knew it could not be very long. Flora, indeed, could have wished it longer, were it not for her charge's sake, as the pleasures of second childhood began to grow weariness. For herself, her daily life, with its little eddies of interest round a chair, and then around a bed; its regular relaxations of air and exercise; its long quiet evenings, when she wrote her daily letters to Arthur, and read the books he sent her; the periodical excitements of his visits, and her drives and walks with him, were as full of happiness as she could dream that earthly life might be. She did not picture to herself what was to come beyond it, any more than she did what heaven was like; only, she longed to be more worthy of it before it came, and tried with reading and study, and learning all he would teach her of the ways and customs of society, to fit herself for being Arthur's wife. As for Arthur, he knew that no effort he could make would ever make him fit to be Flora's husband. It is hard to "climb up the high and rugged barriers" of heaven, but harder far to stoop to it. He hoped that knowing his unworthiness was at least a first step, and the rest of the way he thought she must show him. If he enjoyed the time of waiting less than she, he never betrayed any impatience, and found his consolation when away from her in writing to her, working for her, saving for her. No pledge was asked, no promise given, till two years and more of watching were passed, and then when the funeral was over, and they had returned together to the lonely house, and stood together in the empty room, all Arthur said was: —

"Flora, I know that mother would care for nothing but to have us happy. She would not wish us to wait. How soon shall we be married?"

And Flora answered: "Whenever you please."

Arthur's relations and the Liverpool public in general were not surprised, as they had long accepted the evident fact that "Arthur Butler and Flora Shepherd were keepin' company;" neither were the McCalls. Mr. McCall had growled furiously when he first heard of the arrangement for Mrs. Butler's behalf, declaring it to be a piece of meanness on Arthur's part of which he never could have believed him guilty. "Could n't he hire a trained nurse for the old lady instead of getting it out of Flora? I declare," he wound up, "I'll write, and offer to pay for one myself."

"Flora writes as if she were glad to go," said Ida, tearfully. "Oh dear! she will never come here now!"

"No, I don't believe she will. I suppose when his mother's dead, he'll condescend to marry her, and she'll take him with thanks."

"Hamlin! you must not say such things!"

"Well, well, he's a good fellow enough in his way,— just the kind that girls fall head over ears in love with because they put on airs, while we poor fellows who do our best to please you, have to stand your airs — hey, little madam!"

Ida appeased her husband's wrath by caresses and soft words, suppressing meanwhile some anxieties of her own in the subject; which, however, were laid to rest when she met her sister and Arthur again.

CHAPTER XVIII.

"WHO do you think has bought the house at the corner?" inquired one of the cousins in Miss Curtis's drawing-room. It was late in the autumn, and all the Curtis connection had come back to town, and were running in and out of one another's houses, eager as the Athenians of old to hear and to tell some new thing. No one topic had the slightest chance of monopolizing attention, and the question was speedily submerged in a torrent of talk, — "Smiths going abroad — Joneses come back — Fanny Tiffany really engaged — Nelly Mallory really not — " before some one found breath or time for "The house on the corner, — some one bought it, did you say?"

"Symphony tickets all gone — where are yours? — mine shocking — will not go under the balcony — anything better than too far forward — " ran on the talk.

"Yes, — Arthur Butler has bought it, I hear."

"Nothing to wear — children in rags — perfectly destitute —" buzzed the female portion of the gathering; the persons alluded to not being any indigent protégés, but themselves and their own well-fed, healthy offspring, fresh from rural sports.

"Indeed! Arthur must be doing well."

"He's married, is he not?"

"Yes," said Miss Curtis; "he was married in the spring. Why, did n't you get his cards?"

"Oh, yes, we had some cards, — I don't know what became of them; they had no address on them."

"No, they went abroad directly, so I heard."

By this time the topic of Arthur Butler and his marriage had risen to the top of the wave, and all the duets and trios of conversation merged in one grand scene. Mrs. Curtis remarked that "since they had come to live so near, right in the midst of everybody, she supposed we must call."

"Yes, and send them presents," said Rosamond Perry.

"Rather late in the day, is n't it?" drawled her husband.

"Certainly not," replied the young lady,

decidedly. "Arthur Butler sent me a lovely one when we were married."

"I sent him one as soon as I received the cards," said Miss Curtis.

"Oh, Cousin Rachel, you always do so exactly what you ought! But I am sure it will be a sufficient excuse that they went off so soon."

"Well," acquiesced Tom, lazily, "better late than never."

"I will ask them to the wedding," said Frances Curtis, loftily; "that is, to the church, — I don't know about the house."

"Anybody know anything about her?" asked Tom Perry, who liked news, but was too lazy to pick them up for himself.

"I hear she's some ordinary sort of a girl from that country-place where he came from, — somewhere in New York — what's the name?" said Miss Snow, a purveyor of gossip for genteel society, and a self-constituted toady to Miss Curtis, who did not like her, but thought it her duty to help her, as she was poor and needed it.

"Dear me, what a pity!" said Rosamond.

"Yes," said her husband, "a low match is the ruin of a man. I didn't think Arthur Butler, somehow, was the sort of fellow to do such a thing."

"What kind of a note did she write when you sent them your present?" asked Frances.

"Arthur wrote,—very nicely, as he always does," replied her cousin.

"Very likely she does n't know how to write a note; that is apt to be their stumbling-block," said Miss Snow, who thought she knew enough of the family affairs to be sure that these remarks would please.

"It is a very foolish thing," said Rosamond, "if he has made a mesalliance, for them to take that house. It is always a mistake for a man to try and drag a woman up, when she has n't it in her. Now, Aleck Silsbee showed some sense when he married a shop-girl; he went and lived in Somerville, and went with the people there."

"This girl was the nurse, I believe, who took care of his mother, when she was ill; she died last spring," said Miss Snow.

"She was a clergyman's daughter, the newspapers said," said Miss Curtis, shortly; "Reverend—I forget the name—Shepherd, of some town in New Hampshire."

"That's not saying much," said Rosamond.

"Perhaps she was a trained nurse; some of them are quite lady-like," said Miss Snow, in despair at the dark cloud settling on her patroness's brow; and she did her best to change the subject, — not in time to save herself from the displeasure of Miss Curtis, to whom all these hits were so many stabs. Sophy, she saw, took them with perfect calmness, but then she really believed sometimes that the disappointment had not been so great to Sophy as it was to her. She thought, and rightly, that when she knew him no woman had ever come nearer to Arthur Butler than herself. Though he had been unseen and unmentioned for years, his place had not been — could never be — filled, and the feelings which the chance familiar sound of his name stirred up showed her that he was still dear.

Miss Curtis and Sophy had prolonged their stay abroad to two years and a half; and when they came back it was summer, — every one was scattered; and when they took up the threads of their old life Arthur's was not the only one missing. In spite of all the attractions of the lady's lot, it looked less roseate than a few years ago, when her dreams of her own future linked with Arthur's and Sophy's were so bright. One had disappointed her, and though the other was the same good girl as ever, yet their intercourse, by the necessity of avoiding one prominent subject, and care not to touch on painful allusions, had grown less frank and free than of old. Since their return from abroad they had seen less of each other, and in a less confidential way. The Curtis family had greatly enlarged its borders. Rosamond had two more children, and Frances was going to be married, and Willie's engagement was just announced, and Lucy was coming out this fall; while in the other branches the changes were almost past reckoning. In all these experiences Miss Curtis and Sophy must lend sympathy and help, while, with the inevitable tendency of love to run downward, Sophy's mind was now much taken up with the rising generation of nephews and nieces, while her parents had grown older, and needed her more at home as the other girls married off. Miss Curtis began for the first time in her life to realize the fact that she was growing old herself.

She said nothing more then, but the very next day she quietly walked off to call on Mrs. Arthur Butler. She did not ask Sophy's or any one's company, for she thought that whether her first impressions were pleasant or unpleasant, she would rather have them over by herself. The house was a pretty, new one, finished and fitted to suit the purchaser's taste; and Miss Curtis liked the looks of the drawing-room, though it did not at all resemble that of other newly married couples of her acquaintance; perhaps for that very reason. The furniture was some of it old, all of it good, but it was barely more than necessary in quantity, and there was a marked deficiency of bric-à-brac, dear or cheap. " Not many wedding-presents," she thought; "a pity, but then how should there be!" She knew she had given a silver tea-set, as pretty a one as she could choose; and the Hamlin McCalls, though this she did not know, had spared no expense in the forks and spoons; but these were not gifts that could be displayed without occasion, and there were but few others. Perhaps the room gained by reflecting the individual taste of its owner, rather than the reflected taste of the owner's friends and acquaintances. Almost everything in it had been bought by Arthur himself, from the hour when he had first felt that he could afford to spend a few of his savings in that way, through the later years, when with Flora's image in his mind, he had selected surroundings for her, up to the time when they had chosen a few things together abroad.

"I should know the room was Arthur's if I saw it in Japan!" thought Miss Curtis as she looked around on the pictures, the books, even the writing-things. "I wonder what her taste is like, or if she has any! At any rate, the room looks homelike, and as if she let him live in it."

So short a time did her hostess keep her waiting that she found herself, in the midst of her observations, shaking hands with a young lady who was saying, "I am very glad to see you."

"And I am very glad that I am fortunate enough to find you at home," said Miss Curtis. She tried to add something kind and encouraging to relieve the shyness she thought the young stranger might be feeling, but stopped, suddenly struck silent. It seemed incredible that she should not have heard of Mrs. Arthur Butler before, no matter how low the latter's position, or how far off she lived. She was keenly alive to beauty in all shapes, and Flora was as much more beautiful now than when she had first opened the door for Arthur as four years of life and love could make her. "It is not to be expected," thought Miss Curtis, "that any man could keep from falling in love with such a girl as this! — but it is a pity, — it must have made him overlook so much else!"

"Arthur has often spoken to me about you, and all your great kindness to him," said Flora. Miss Curtis could not tell why these simple words gave her so much pleasure, but she rallied from her surprise, and answered: —

"I may call myself, I hope, an old friend of your husband's, though we have not met so much lately."

"Arthur has missed you; and he hoped, when we came to live so near you, that he should see you sometimes."

"I hope we shall meet a great deal," said Miss Curtis, her astonishment increasing at the rashness with which she was making advances at the very outset. She checked herself, and as she looked about for some suggestion to change the subject, her eye fell on a chromo-lithograph in a slightly worn frame, hanging above an old-fashioned writing-desk, evidently belonging to the mistress of the house.

"I dare say you remember that," said Flora, following her glance; "it was one that you once sent Mrs. Butler by Arthur; it always hung in her room, and when she was shut up so long she enjoyed looking at it so much."

"I am very glad,—and I am glad you like to keep it here."

"Yes, I grew very fond of it. When we went abroad Arthur took me straight to Florence to see the original, and all the others of his that we could."

"I suppose you had a delightful journey; but of course you did."

"We enjoyed it very much; but we were glad to get home. It is so long since Arthur had any home, you know."

"Your home looks like a charming one, and I hope you will be very happy in it. You must let me say that I have always thought that Arthur's wife would be a very fortunate woman."

She began to feel that her youthful hostess's beauty was rendered almost too impressive by the gentle gravity that seemed a little strange in her position, and longed to see her face lighted by a smile. But perhaps some lurking memories of her own made her own speech earnest in tone; and Flora replied, "I am sure of that," in like manner.

Miss Curtis, irresistibly attracted, went on:

"Now that we are both settled I hope that you and Arthur will come and dine with me sociably,—with no one else but perhaps a relative or two,—let us say on Thursday, if you have no engagement. We can learn to know each other so much sooner, if you will come; don't try to call first, if you are very busy."

"Thank you very much," said Flora, "we have been nowhere. It is so short a time since Arthur lost his mother;" and she looked down on her severely plain but exquisitely made black dress.

"Oh, don't let that prevent you!" interrupted her visitor. "You see," she went on, "it is not as if you knew more people here. It is not good for you to be entirely shut up. Most people have relations among whom they can go about a little; can't you consider me as one? I should be so pleased if you would treat me as your aunt, if you only had one here."

"Thank you; since you are so kind, we shall be very glad to come," answered Flora, immediately. "It will be a great pleasure to Arthur, as well as to me."

Miss Curtis, struck with consternation at her own temerity in adopting another niece on the spot, was yet forced to go on with, "And would you not like to come and read with me and one or two others on Wednesday mornings? Only a few intimate friends. We have not begun our meetings yet, but we propose to have Signor Corticelli read Dante to us in the original. I do not know whether you read Italian?" She paused, again alarmed at the involuntary throwing open of her most inner circle. "But some of us do not, and will follow with a translation," she added, fearful of being supposed to assume superiority.

"You are very kind; I should enjoy it very much, if I did not keep the others back; and Arthur will be very glad that I have the chance. He likes me to read Italian, but I never had any real teaching, except for the little time we were in Italy last spring."

"Had you studied it before?"

"Arthur sent me the books, and I got on as well as I could alone. I had learned a little Latin, and that helped of course."

"You must be very persevering."

"Arthur was so pleased, I could not help being."

"Well!" thought Miss Curtis, "I wonder how long Arthur has been educating this child!" A burning desire seized her to know, — it might help to clear up some points on which she must ever be doubtful; and yielding to a sudden impulse and angry with herself the next moment for having yielded to what she felt to be intrusive curiosity, she said: " You and Arthur were engaged a long time, were you not?

"I do not know," replied Flora, with so much simplicity that Miss Curtis, while she felt that she had received a rebuff, could not suppose that it was intended for one. Flora, who really did not know, saw no reason for not saying so; but she thought she ought to show more confidence in so old a friend, and continued, " We met each other first four years ago last spring."

Miss Curtis rapidly travelled backwards in her mind. " It was destiny!" she thought, " and that is all that can be said. I only wonder why he waited so long!" but she could ask no more questions. The past had best be buried, with all its regrets. She made no effort in bidding Flora farewell in the very kindest manner, and it was a comfort — she could hardly understand why it was so great a one — to receive as kind a response. They parted, it might be called affectionately, and Miss Curtis, as she trod the pavements, marvelled at herself, and thought she must be bewitched. She went into her cousin's, thinking that to formulate her impressions in words might help her to be more sure of them.

"I have been to call on Mrs. Arthur Butler," she announced to the very fair representation of the family who were present.

"Oh, have you? how exciting! What is she like?" asked Rosamond.

"I do not know," replied Miss Curtis, glad to borrow Flora's answer.

"Is she pretty?" asked Frances.

"Pretty!" repeated Miss Curtis, in supreme disgust; "pretty? no, indeed."

"Dear me!" said Rosamond, "I never thought that Arthur Butler would marry an ugly girl! I should really like to see them together; it would be funny."

"I am sure," said Frances, "Richard Wilkinson, who met them the other day, said she was pretty."

"Richard Wilkinson calls every girl pretty that is not actually deformed," said Rosamond, scornfully.

Miss Curtis turned from them in lofty pity for their ignorance. "They are coming to dine with me on Thursday," she said to their silent elder sister; "will you come, Sophy, and meet them? I think," she added, "that you will like her."

Sophy accepted very pleasantly. She had none of the proverbial fury of a woman scorned against Arthur, and felt none of the natural feminine satisfaction in his wife's possible plainness or awkwardness. She would have liked her successful rival to be a worthy one.

The joys of our maturer age are oftenest those which youth despises, even when it possesses them; and when Sophy's heart was thrilling with just recognized love, responding to a preference so plainly shown by Arthur Butler, it might have sounded cheerless enough to her to be told that one of the principal sources of her future happiness was to be a very tender and life-long friendship with Arthur Butler's future wife; but so it was, and the friendship was all the stronger because so much less was expressed than was felt; because it rested on an unseen foundation of forgiveness, and sacrifice none the less real that it was compulsory. Arthur was not without his part in the latter; for Flora, as he had foreseen, was never to know the secret he would fain have told her.

Miss Curtis, too, found that Arthur's society and his successes and his family life were still to make one of her life's best satisfactions, though differently, indeed, from what her hope had pictured. She was relieved, if somewhat ashamed, to find how soon she could dearly love the unconscious interloper; perhaps the more because about Flora there was a slight veil of mystery which heightened her charm. No one could be in the company of Mr. and Mrs. Arthur Butler without being sure, not only that they loved each other with an entire and perfect devotion, but that their mutual sympathy was so profound that the exclusiveness of love gave way in them to a union in their friendships which gave these a double fervor; and no one knew this better than Miss Curtis; but all this being true, surely Flora should look happier.

"Not that she looks unhappy," thought Miss Curtis, as for the hundredth time she studied the calm, pathetic sweetness of her young neighbor's expression, "but if I were a man I don't think I should like my wife to look like that. To be sure," she always wound up, "Arthur seems satisfied, and if he is, surely every one else ought to be — only — "

Arthur was satisfied. Flora was his; and to know how entirely she was so stimulated him as well. He knew that if she were not happy it was because there must be something better than happiness, and that she had found it. He could wait for time to bring all lesser blessings too, and for her own babies in her arms to awake the sleeping smiles about her lovely mouth.

THE END.

www.ingramcontent.com/pod-product-compliance
Lightning Source LLC
Chambersburg PA
CBHW030016240426
43672CB00007B/982